NOR

Tom Pocock belongs to a naval family which has its roots in the Norfolk that Nelson knew. During a Fleet Street career of half a century, he has reported on the end of the Second World War as well as Vietnam and Northern Ireland. He is the author of fifteen books, including a biography of Nelson which was runner-up for the Whitbread Biography Prize in 1987.

Pimlico County History Guides
(General editor: Christopher Hibbert)

Already published:

Bedfordshire by Simon Houfe
Dorset by Richard Ollard
Somerset by Shirley Toulson
Suffolk by Miles Jebb
Sussex by Desmond Seward

Forthcoming:

Cambridgeshire by Ross Clark
Lincolnshire by Henry Thorrold
Oxfordshire by John Steane

NORFOLK

TOM POCOCK

with a Foreword by Christopher Hibbert

A PIMLICO COUNTY HISTORY GUIDE

To the Bowers family, formerly
of North Creake and Norwich,
past and present

PIMLICO

An imprint of Random House
20 Vauxhall Bridge Road, London SW1V 2SA

Random House Australia (Pty) Ltd
20 Alfred Street, Milsons Point, Sydney
New South Wales 2061, Australia

Random House New Zealand Ltd
18 Poland Road, Glenfield
Auckland 10, New Zealand

Random House South Africa (Pty) Ltd
PO Box 337, Bergvlei, South Africa

Random House UK Ltd Reg. No. 954009

First published by Pimlico 1995

1 3 5 7 9 10 8 6 4 2

Papers used by Random House UK Limited are natural,
recyclable products made from wood grown in sustainable
forests. The manufacturing processes conform to the
environmental regulations of the country of origin

Typeset by Deltatype Ltd, Ellesmere Port, Cheshire
Printed and bound in Great Britain by
Mackays of Chatham plc, Chatham, Kent

ISBN 0-7126-5154-3

Contents

Acknowledgements

I must thank many Norfolk people, past and present, for their contributions to this book. Notably, in the past, I am grateful to my mother for introducing me to Norfolk as a child and for passing on to me her love of the county and its independent-minded people. Amongst others to whom I must refer in the past tense are Bishop Aubrey Aitken, the Revd Howard Banister, Mr Allen Bell, Canon and Mrs Boughey, Brigadier Frank Brayne, Miss Dorothy Falkner, Mr Bill Haines, Mr James Riches, Mr Richard Rudyard-Helpman and my father, Guy Pocock, who was as stirred by the story of Robert Kett as I have been and wrote about him in a book of essays.

Amongst our contemporaries, I am grateful to Mr Philip Athill, Mr Ben Burgess, Lord Blake, Commander Mark Cheyne, Mr Tom Cook, Mrs Charlotte Crawley, Lady Margaret Douglas-Home, Miss Audrey Earle, Mr Derek Edwards, Miss Bridget Everitt, Commander Andrew Fountaine, Mrs Maisie Gee, Mr Bryan Hall, Lady Harrod, Mr Dominick Harrod, Judge Adrian Head, Mr Richard Hough, the Revd Cecil Isaacson, Mr Tim Matthews, Mr Bernard Phillips, Mr Michael Riviere, Mr Charles Roberts, Mr and Mrs John Thompson, Dr Peter and Dr Susanna Wade Martins, Miss Norma Watt, Mr Peter Wickham and Mr Les Winter.

In documentary and pictorial research my thanks are due to the Directors and staff of the Norfolk County Library, the Norfolk Record Office, the Norwich Castle Museum, the Norfolk Museums Service.

I am grateful to Mr Michael Riviere for allowing me to quote the whole of his poem *Felbrigg*, published by the Mandeville Press; to Mr Kevin Crossley-Holland for allowing quotations from his poems *Billy* and *The Great Painter*, published by Hutchinson & Co, Ltd.; and to Mr Richard Hough for quotations from his *One Boy's War* published by William Heinemann Ltd. Simon and Schuster Ltd kindly gave permission for me to quote from Nigel McCrery's book *The Vanished Battalion* and John Murray (Publishers) Ltd have allowed me to quote from Sir Osbert Lancaster's *All Done from Memory* and Sir John Betjeman's *Lord Cozens Hardy* in his *Collected Poems*.

My thanks are also due to the Earl of Leicester and the Trustees of the Holkham Estate for giving Dona Haycraft permission to photograph Holkham Park and to Mr D. A. Edwards of the Landscape Archaeology Section of the Norfolk Museums Service and to Aerial Photography Publications for permission to reproduce photographs of Warham fort and Norwich.

Mr Christopher Hibbert, the editor of this series, Mr Will Sulkin, its publisher, and Mr Euan Cameron, my editor, have all been generous with practical help and encouragement.

Foreword

'Sir Nöel Coward's familiar quip about the flatness of Norfolk', Tom Pocock observes, 'blends with a general misconception that it is a dull, uninspiring county of worthies and yokels', a county, according to another popular misconception, remarkable for little other than being 'full of parsons and oak trees', or, as Horace Walpole put it, occupied by 'roast beef fashioned in human form'.

Tom Pocock is just the man to correct such idle and comical misjudgements. The grandson of a Norfolk clergyman who became Bishop of Thetford, and the son of the author of a novel set in a cathedral city which is clearly Norwich, he himself spent his holidays in the county as a boy and still stays there for several weeks each year, while three of his books are biographies of Norfolk men – Horatio Nelson, son of the rector of Burnham Thorpe, William Hoste, Nelson's protégé born at Ingoldisthorpe, and Rider Haggard, son of the squire of West Bradenham. And in this new, delightfully written book his knowledge of Norfolk and his affection for it are evident on every page.

His Norfolk is a place which, when seen from the air, is 'painted in shades of green and brown. These are rich, healthy colours, so different from the arid yellow, vivid emerald or ash grey of the world's deserts, swamps and mountains. The colouring is symbolic of the prosperity it indicates, for the riches of Norfolk have always been in its soil', a soil ideal 'for the growing of crops and the grazing of sheep and cattle, the foundation of its wealth and of the powerful families who farmed its great estates and built its mansions'. It is a place, too, of wonderful sea-scapes such as those which Nelson saw as a boy on the coast near his father's parsonage, 'sometimes

ix

blue, sometimes grey . . . often flecked with sails, occasionally crowded as when a long-awaited change of wind released a fleet of colliers from the Tyne, or the herring fleet sailed north from Great Yarmouth, or a brisk south-westerly bore a flock of merchantmen to or from the Thames and the Baltic'.

Long before Nelson's time this part of the English coast had a small harbour wherever a river ran into the sea, and every harbour had at some time or other been plundered by the longships of the Vikings on their way to pillage the settlements further inland. Many of these and subsequent invaders remained in the lands which they had come to ravage and loot; and in time the people of what became Norfolk developed those characteristics described by the historian, Lord Blake, himself a Norfolk man, educated in Norwich and now living in Brundall. They are 'largely Scandinavian', he says, 'or Dutch, which is very similar, for there is a lot of Dutch influence in the county. Norfolk people tend to be reserved and suspicious of "foreigners", by which they mean people from other English counties . . . Until the railway age Norfolk was very remote from London.' Indeed, it was far easier to go by boat to Holland than by coach to the Bull and Mouth in St Martin's-le-Grand in the City; and, of course, as Tom Pocock reminds us, Norfolk was 'not on the way to anywhere'. Nelson, who so often raised cheers in the county of his birth by declaring himself so proud to be a Norfolk man and who never entirely lost his Norfolk accent, used to speak of Norfolk almost as though it were a place separate from the rest of England; and this sense of isolation from the lands to the west helped to develop a tradition of independence of spirit and of political and religious dissent.

This tradition of dissent, epitomised in the career of the author of *The Rights of Man*, the radical journalist Thomas Paine, son of a Quaker corset-maker from Thetford, had, however, rarely overcast the pride which Norfolk country people took in their beautiful churches. Villages might still bear names indicative of a pre-Christian past when the gods of the Norsemen were held in awe and reverence here – Thornton, Thornage, Thursford, Thurton and Thurgarden all commemorate the Norse god of thunder – but in villages such as these in the Norfolk Marshland country can be found churches of such beauty and diversity, so rich in medieval art, that even the Suffolk 'wool churches' seem almost commonplace by comparison. In John Betjeman's *Guide to English Parish Churches* there are more listed as being of special interest or aesthetic merit in Norfolk than in any other English county except Lincolnshire, Yorkshire and Suffolk. The sheer number of them is astonishing. In Norwich alone there were already twenty-one by the end of the eleventh century when the population of the city was 5,500; there are now, in addition to the majestic, mainly Norman cathedral, thirty-two, including St Peter Mancroft, described in Sir John Betjeman's book as 'the finest of the large town churches of the fifteenth century'.

Almost a thousand churches were built in Norfolk between the eleventh and sixteenth centuries, far more than in any other county in England, some of them as small as the little All Saints at Waterden, others as grandly magnificent as St Peter and St Paul at Salle, in C. L. S. Linnell's opinion, 'not only the most marvellous church in a county of marvellous churches but one of the most beautiful in all England'.

As with churches so with the country houses, Norfolk has a rich abundancy, varying in style and period from the partly Norman fortified prebendary manor house, Welle Manor Hall, and the late fifteenth-century moated Oxburgh Hall, to Blickling Hall, one of England's greatest Jacobean houses, the seventeenth-century Felbrigg Hall with its beautiful Georgian interiors, the Georgian Gothic Beeston Hall, and two of the most imposingly grand Palladian houses in England, Holkham Hall and Houghton Hall, neither of them far from the Queen's ponderous Victorian house at Sandringham, bought with 7,000 acres in the 1860s for £220,000 for King Edward VII, then Prince of Wales, whose guests played baccarat every night in the over-furnished rooms and danced in the great hall to the music of a barrel organ.

Such country houses in the county were occupied by an ever-changing galaxy of Norfolk families whose achievements, fortunes and foibles are so admirably described in this book. At Holkham, designed by William Kent, lived Thomas Coke, the great farmer who introduced Devon cattle and Southdown sheep to Norfolk, made the rotation of crops compulsory in all his tenancy agreements, reclaimed salt-marshes and held back the sea by planting the dunes so thickly and successfully that he was known as 'King Pine' as well as 'Coke of Norfolk'. South of Holkham at Houghton – designed for Britain's first Prime Minister, Sir Robert Walpole, by Colen Campbell and Thomas Ripley with interiors by William Kent – lived the third Earl of Orford, Walpole's grandson, a highly eccentric man who shared the house with his mistress, a former maidservant, and devoted himself to drinking and gambling, once arranging a race from Norwich to London of five turkeys against five geese and driving about the country-side in a phaeton drawn by two pairs of red deer.

Eccentricity, it seems, has been a notable trait in the Norfolk character for centuries. The county has certainly produced a remarkable number of great men and women, famous sailors and statesmen, writers and painters. Among its heroines are Boudicca and Edith Cavell; its philanthropists include Elizabeth Fry and Jeremiah Colman. Robert Kett, the sixteenth-century rebel leader, came from Wymondham, Matthew Parker, Queen Elizabeth I's Archbishop of Canter-bury, was born in Norwich, Charles Townshend, the statesman, at Raynham Hall to which he returned when his political career was over to devote himself to farming and to the cultivation of turnips, a favourite subject, so it was said, of his conversation in later years. Yet – from the seventeenth-century physician, Sir Thomas Browne, author of *Religio Medici*, who kept, amidst his myriad of curiosities a stork and an eagle which he fed on cats and puppies, to the Revd Harold Davidson, Rector of Stiffkey, who, accused of immoral practices with more than a thousand young women, mostly prostitutes, was defrocked in Norwich Cathedral and was thereafter killed by a lion while preaching from the animal's cage at Skegness – Norfolk eccentrics are legion, there having always been, as Tom Pocock says, a strong inclination among

Norfolk people 'to "do different", perhaps because of their long history of invasion and alien rule'.

A characteristic example of these eccentrics was Rider Haggard's father, Sir William, who took his duties as squire very seriously, stepping into the middle of the nave when any parishioners arrived late in church and brandishing a very large old watch in their faces. He always read the Lessons and when coming upon such lists of obscure names as appear in chapter ten of the Book of Genesis, he would return to the beginning and read them all out again in case he had got any of them wrong. At the end of the service he would allow no one to leave the church until he had himself proceeded slowly to the porch where he would watch the departing congregation, counting them like sheep.

His son, the novelist, who lived at Ditchingham House, thus movingly described the view he loved to contemplate from his windows across the Waveney Valley:

> I have travelled a great way about the world in my time and studied much scenery, but I do not remember anything more quietly and consistently beautiful than this view . . . For the most part of the year the plain below is golden with gorse, but it is not on this alone that the sight depends for its beauty, or on the green of the meadows and the winding river edged with lush marshes that in spring are spotted by yellow marigolds and purple with myriads of cuckoo flowers. They all contribute to it, as do the grazing cattle, the gabled distant roofs and the church spires, but I think that the prospect owes its peculiar charm to the constant changes of light that sweep across its depths. At every season of the year, at every hour of the day it is beautiful, but always with a different beauty.

CHRISTOPHER HIBBERT

NORFOLK

Burnham Overy Staithe
Burnham Market
Blakene
Morston
Scolt Head
Holkham
Stiffkey
Thornham Brancaster
Wells-next-the-Sea
Langha
Hunstanton
Ringstead
Burnham Thorpe
North Creake
Wighton
Heacham
Docking
South Creake
Little Walsingham
Southgate
Bircham Newton
Syderstone
Fakenham
Dersingham
Houghton
Stibbard
Sandringham
Babingley
Harpley
Great Ryburgh
Castle Rising
Great Massingham
Gately
Twyfo
Roydon
Tittleshall
West Lynn
KING'S LYNN
Rougham
Mileham
North Elmham
Terrington St Clement
Gayton
Litcham
Beeston
East Winch
Castle Acre
Newton
Wendling
Pentney Narborough
South Acre
Tilney St Lawrence
Nar
East Dereha
Wisbech
Shouldham
Marham
Swaffham
Bradenham
Cockley Cley
Ashill
Outwell
Downham Market
Hilborough
Hingha
Great Ouse
Oxborough
Watton
Stoke Ferry
Foulden
Wissey
Didlington
Hilgay
Southery
Methwold
Mundford
Feltwell
Grime's Graves
Wretham
Weeting
East Harling
Thetford
Kenningha
Little Ouse

CAMBRIDGESHIRE

The Wash

SUFF

Prologue

Norfolk is a county of strong character and distinctive attitudes. But, unlike some such places around the world – Wales and Tibet come to mind – it is not a natural stronghold. There is no mountain fastness, no dangerous sea to keep it inviolate. East Anglia spread before the invader from the east with irresistible appeal, as accessible as it was fertile. Over the centuries, Norfolk people met the shock of repeated invasions from Rome, Scandinavia, Germany, the Low Countries and Normandy, staggered from the onslaught, then absorbed the invaders and turned them into Norfolk people with characteristics that became and remained recognisable.

Since there were no mineral resources in the county, natives and settlers (the latter becoming, in time, the former) lived mostly by farming and fishing. As the ownership of land became increasingly concentrated, a social hierarchy evolved and interlocked with that of all England, albeit at a distance. Once the disrupted population had absorbed the latest incomers and settled into such patterns, it found itself remarkably isolated; from the coastal regions it was easier to reach Holland than to negotiate great forests, fens and heaths on a journey to, say, Winchester, and, of course, Norfolk was not on the way to anywhere. This, combined with so strong a strain of Scandinavian genes, and developed a character so distinct from that of England to the west of the woods and wetlands that Norfolk developed an independence of spirit. It bred political and religious dissent, supporting several rural revolts, Parliament against the King in the Civil War and Puritanism that later found expression in Methodism and Quakerism. One of its most forceful sons was the radical Thomas Paine, author of the book and the slogan, *The Rights of Man.* It became the seed-bed of agricultural innovation: two of its other great men were farmers – 'Turnip' Townshend and 'Coke of Norfolk'. It produced an original school of painting: if ever artists drew inspiration from their surroundings it was the painters of the Norwich School. No wonder that the hero of the whole nation has for two centuries been an idiosyncratic, tough yet vulnerable, vain yet humble contradiction of a man, Horatio Nelson.

It was he who gave us an idea of the sheer size and diversity of the county by his use of a preposition. Instead of saying, on leaving his ship, that he was going to Norfolk, as we might, the naval hero would write, '*Boreas* will soon be paid off, then we shall come into Norfolk directly', or, often, that 'I would fain go into Norfolk.' The word 'into' suggests a country rather than a county. For him, as for others, it was also a haven.

This is a personal view of Norfolk history, so the writer's vantage-point needs to be mentioned. It has spanned most of the latter three-quarters of the twentieth century, reaching back to its beginning through the stories with which he grew up. My grandfather, Jack Bowers, was a Norfolk clergyman, partly Scottish – his father was born in Elgin – and had first seen East Anglia as a Cambridge undergraduate; his sister had married a Thorndike (the sister of his fellow-curate at St Mary Redcliffe in Bristol), who claimed East Anglian ancestry; and he married a Beaumont from Coggeshall in Essex, one of whose ancestors had arrived there from Normandy with Duke William. Jack Bowers had been a canon and Archdeacon of Gloucester, and, in 1903, he came to Norfolk as Rector of North Creake, Archdeacon of Lynn and Bishop of Thetford. In the remaining twenty-three years of his life, he became, by all accounts, immensely popular: a jolly, wise man with a deep bass voice and a common touch. Perhaps it is not surprising that the actress Dame Sybil Thorndike should have been his niece.

His only daughter, my mother, lived with her parents first at North Creake and then in The Close at Norwich. She was married there in the cathedral, where I was christened by my grandfather. He passed on to me through his daughter many

Norfolk friendships and an equal regard for all; for example, he himself was particularly popular with Norfolk railwaymen and the royal family; his friendships included great landowners and country vergers; he fitted well into Norfolk's tradition of accepting each person on their merits, a tradition which, I am glad to see, is now followed by his great-grand-daughters.

My holidays were spent, from the age of seven, in north-west Norfolk; my wartime experiences included sea-time with motor torpedo-boats based on Great Yarmouth; post-war, the Norfolk holidays were resumed and then, for sixteen years, I owned (latterly with my wife, herself a great-great-niece of Bishop Bowers) a small house in Burnham Overy Staithe, a village where we continue to spend several weeks a year. Links with the county have been further strengthened by my writing books about Norfolkmen: Horatio Nelson, William Hoste and Rider Haggard.

At one time a Norfolk friend and I had a running joke about the desirability of a Unilateral Declaration of Independence for the county. Times have changed and so has Norfolk; its strong character has been diluted by yet another wave of settlement and UDI no longer seems so appropriate as it did thirty years ago. But the friend and I still recognise a person, an attitude, or an event as being particularly 'Norfolk'. Now, as always, this land tempts the settler, so will it soon be changed beyond recognition by the latest mass-migration, or will the migrants themselves become recognisably native as have so many before them?

Norfolk always appears the essence of fecundity and peace. Yet, because it has always seemed to spread out defenceless before its envious enemies, who aspired to settlement, it was formed by war and the threat of invasion from the east has recurred down the centuries: where Romans built coastal forts, the Royal Air Force built airfields. So, in looking at aspects of the county, rather than at its evolution as an entity, it is as appropriate as it may be surprising to start with war.

I
War

Nowhere seems more deeply sunk in tranquillity than the long Norfolk shore when little waves curl upon the wide sands. Even when gales blow out of the North Sea, the coastal villages are protected against the surf by dunes and saltings, and even the crumbling cliffs between Weybourne and Happisburgh fight a stubborn, if losing, action against the invading seas.

But beneath the calm lurks foreboding. As a boy on holiday, camping among the dunes of Scolt Head, I was always aware of a dangerous undertow. In the 1930s, distant thumps from the anti-aircraft artillery range at Weybourne were one reminder; my elders' talk of friends 'lost at Jutland', directly over the eastern horizon, was another. In the imagination, the German battlecruisers that had shelled Great Yarmouth were still out there in the mist, held back only by the resolution of the Royal Navy – 'Ready, Aye, Ready!' we were always told – which was out there, too.

When Nelson was a boy in Burnham Thorpe, he must have felt much the same as I did at that age. The chalk crest above the shallow valley, where he lived, was called Beacon Hill for that had been where beacons had warned of invasion by the Danes, who had burned the churches and been fought on a slope, further up the valley, still called Bloodgate. Invaders came over the horizon, that line ruled between the shoulders of the downs; later, the French might come from there, too. Then, when my mother lived nearby, it would be the Germans; and in my time, too. Thoughts of war were never far away; nor, sometimes, war itself. It had always been so.

The threat to the desirable countries of Europe has always come from the east. The first invaders could walk from the

4

plains of continental Europe before the seas isolated England six or seven millennia before Christ. The east coast remained vulnerable, awaiting invaders who had developed ships able to carry them across the North Sea. Off the Norfolk coast there were dangerous sandbanks but these were of little risk to shallow-draught longships from Scandinavia which would slide on to the sandy beaches and nose up the creeks and rivers.

There was danger on land, too, from invaders who had come ashore on the south coast and also from indigenous enemies. This approach was more difficult for Norfolk was shielded by thick forest growing in the clay of the south and by fens in the west. There were, however, two possible overland routes for invasion. One was a coastal strip between the sea and the forest; the other was a belt of chalk downland, five to ten miles wide, running from the heartland of Wessex north-east, past what is now Newmarket, into 'High Norfolk' in the north-west of the county and known as the Icknield Way.

Settlers, if not invaders, came from north-eastern France, the Low Countries and Germany and, although there are no records of major warfare, defensive earthworks remain, suggesting that they were built for good reason. There was inter-tribal rivalry, too, and war between two of the most powerful tribes in England, the Catuvellauni of western East Anglia and the Iceni of Norfolk, was about to break out when, in AD 43, the Romans landed on the south coast.

Brave, indeed ferocious, as they were, the British tribes could not stand against the shock tactics of the armoured phalanxes of the Roman legions and, once the Catuvellauni were defeated, the Iceni made peace, retaining nominal independence in return for an oath of loyalty to Rome. As was customary under such circumstances, the Romans assumed that King Prasutagus of the Iceni would leave his land to the Emperor of Rome. In the event, he died and bequeathed only half to Nero, the rest being kept in his own family. Then the Roman army, ordered to collect the expected legacy, invaded the Iceni kingdom, captured and flogged the King's widow Boudicca and raped her two daughters. As soon as she was released, the Queen set about raising a revolt, supported by another East Anglian tribe, the Trinovantes.

Boudicca's (or Boadicea's) rebellion has grown into one of the romantic legends of British history, illustrated by the three bronze ladies on their chariot, with scythe-blades protruding from its hubcaps, which can be seen at Westminster Bridge in London. In fact, like most civil wars, it was singularly nasty. After the Iceni took Colchester (then Camulodunum), they enjoyed an orgy of torturing the captured Romano-British families before pouring along the road to sack St Albans (Verulamium) and then London (Londinium) itself.

The Romans had stationed four legions in Britain: one in Lincoln, one in Gloucester, and two were on an expedition to North Wales. All reacted with speed when couriers galloped into their camps. First, the 9th Legion marched out of Lincoln to intercept the Iceni's advance on London, only to be ambushed and almost wiped out. The senior Roman officer, Suetonius, was in Wales and he rode ahead with his cavalry in the hope of saving London, sending a courier to Gloucester to summon that legion to reinforce him. He reached London with only his cavalry, just ahead of the Iceni, but, realising that he could not hope to hold the city, abandoned it to a terrible fate.

The Roman commander at Gloucester had not responded to Suetonius's command, so it was with his two legions, his cavalry and some auxiliaries that Suetonius finally intercepted Boudicca. Outnumbered by ten to one, he drew up his legions in a strong defensive position with a forest to protect their rear and open country in front, and it was across this that the wild horde of the Iceni charged. Again and again the Roman cavalry and archers broke up the onslaughts and, when the Iceni began to tire, it was they who tramped forward in tight formations behind walls of shields. Roman discipline prevailed and the Iceni, encumbered by their families, baggage train and loot, were massacred in their turn; Boudicca took poison. The senior officer of the legion at Gloucester, who had not responded to the call, fell on his sword. The site of the battle has never been identified, but Amesbury Banks in Essex has been suggested. Perhaps it was at one of those villages in southern England with a name beginning Ick– ? After all, the Iceni gave their name to Ickburgh in Norfolk and Ickworth in Suffolk; East Anglians have long talked about 'Ickenies'.

So the Romans occupied Norfolk, crushing the social and military structure of the Iceni. The capital was moved from Thetford in the south to the new fortified town of Venta Icenorum, at what is now Caistor St Edmund, outside Norwich. They built military roads and developed old tracks – notably the Peddar's Way, which crossed Norfolk from south to north-west reaching the sea at Thornham, where they built a signal station to communicate with the garrison at Lincoln across the Wash. Nearby they built a coastal fort at Brancaster, where the village itself still stands in a Roman grid-pattern, to guard the ferry that plied across the Wash from Holme-next-the-Sea, another grid-pattern village. These coastal forts, and others at Stiffkey and further down the coast, were not only garrisons but bases for fast fighting-galleys to counter the increasing number of raids from the sea by Scots and Saxons.

At the beginning of the fifth century, threats to Rome of barbarian invasion from the east brought about the evacuation of the legions from Britain. The defence of the island was now in the hands of mercenaries unable to withstand the mounting strength of raiders from the sea. In the third decade of the century the last Roman soldiers left Britain and the Dark Ages had begun.

As the legions withdrew, new settlers arrived. They were Saxons from north-west Germany and they crossed the sea cautiously in big rowing galleys, hugging the coast of the Continent before daring the crossing to the cliffs of Kent.

Pulling north across the Thames estuary to the islands, creeks and the long, open beaches of East Anglia, they began to look for land suitable for settlement. Once ashore, there was seen to be ample space; they were good farmers and herdsmen and they prospered. During the relative peace that followed, Christianity reached Britain at the end of the sixth century. Within a hundred years, a Norfolk see had its administrative base at North Elmham, where a cathedral was built. Norwich and Thetford became increasingly important mercantile centres and the arts flourished.

Anglo-Saxon Norfolk was, however, in the weakest of the three Anglo-Saxon kingdoms, East Anglia, which was constantly at war with the other two, Mercia and Wessex. The most immediate threat to East Anglia came from Mercia and, to defend the Icknield Way, huge earthworks were thrown up north-west of Cambridge, notably the Devil's Dyke. Tribal warfare was the norm in all countries; far more dangerous were raids that came from the sea.

In AD 789, the Vikings first erupted from Scandinavia. The younger sons of chieftains, lacking the lands inherited by their elder brothers, driven by population pressure or crop failure to seek new, fertile land, or by blood feuds, and hankering after the warmer climate of the south, sailed on their first voyage of aggressive exploration. Their long, low ocean-going ships – called longships, or dragon-ships because of their fierce figureheads – were driven by a single, large, square sail and by oars; unlike the Saxons, they did not creep along the coastline, but came up over the horizon with shocking surprise; modern trials have shown that they could sail at a speed of twelve knots.

The Vikings' first target was the monastery of Lindisfarne, which they sacked, but not for nearly half a century did they turn their attention to East Anglia. The first raids were for plunder, often from monasteries and churches, which were seen as centres of wealth and were undefended. Soon their raids penetrated deeper inland, up the rivers, then by mounting horses and sweeping far inland and again achieving surprise. They had already broken up the structure of East Anglian society when, in 869, they decided to stay ashore for the winter and made camp far from the sea at Thetford.

The Anglo-Saxons fought back against what they called the *aesemann* and the *flottmann* – pirates and Vikings – words preserved in the names of the villages of Ashmanlaugh and Newton Flotman; many villages in Norfolk and Denmark have remarkably similar names. Next year, King Edmund of

East Anglia was besieged at Framlingham in Suffolk but seems to have escaped and made his way to Norwich, only to be captured nearby by the Vikings. Tied to a tree, he was shot through with arrows, then beheaded; later to be canonised and remembered in the names of Bury St Edmunds, churches and schools.

For nearly two centuries, the Vikings – mostly Danes – remained in East Anglia despite the ebb and flow of battles with the Anglo-Saxons further south. They were defeated by King Alfred but then prevailed over Ethelred the Unready, who had constantly tried to bribe them to stay away, in the great battle at Maldon.

The Danes bequeathed more than fair hair and blue eyes to Norfolk. They left place-names – notably those ending with -*by*, -*dale*, -*holme*, -*toft* or -*thorpe* and, in towns, ending with -*gate*, meaning street – and villages named after others in Denmark. They also left an abiding fear of strangers from the sea, and when, as a child, Horatio Nelson was told about the wicked French by his mother, at the back of their minds were inherited memories eight centuries old.

The watershed year was, of course, 1066. Then King Harold defeated the Scandinavian Norsemen and was himself defeated and killed by those who had settled in France a century before and were now called Normans. It took time for the Norman Conquest to reach Norfolk but, when it did so, it was efficient, the invaders staking out and pinning down the county with garrisons and dividing it between ecclesiastical institutions.

Peace was not easily imposed. The Danes pressed their own claims to East Anglia with an expeditionary force which landed in Suffolk and attacked Norwich. But they were not the warriors they had been and were beaten back. Their raid did coincide, however, with an indigenous rising in the fens led by the guerrilla leader who became legendary as Hereward the Wake. The Normans had to mount major naval and military operations before he was driven from his stronghold on the Isle of Ely and into hiding.

Wars fought on Norfolk soil during the next six centuries

were civil. It was obvious to the Normans that this might be so and to meet such contingencies their garrisons were housed in massive stone castles, notably at Norwich, Thetford, Castle Acre and Castle Rising. The social system imposed on England by the Normans created a pattern of land-ownership and taxation against which both the natives and avaricious landowners rebelled. The most spontaneous of demonstrations was what became known as the Peasants' Revolt of 1381, when the south and east of England protested against the introduction of a hated poll tax and the conditions of serfdom. Trouble began in Norfolk on the day that crowds of protesters from Kent and Essex poured into London and their leader, Wat Tyler, confronted King Richard II at Smithfield only to be struck down and killed in the presence of the Lord Mayor of London.

A mob from Essex, joined by groups of Norfolkmen, threatened to burn Thetford, then moved into the west of the county. Quickly, the rising spread, breaking out in different parts and concentrating on the houses of tax-collectors and magistrates. There was much burning of tax documents, looting and a few murders before the Bishop of Norwich, Henry Despenser, a warrior-priest who had fought in Flanders, launched a counter-offensive. Rallying the Norfolk gentry and their tenants, he dispersed the marauding protesters, just when they were demoralised by the arrival of news of Wat Tyler's death. Once the local leader, Geoffrey Litster, had himself been executed, and their delegation to present a petition to the King intercepted by the ruthless Bishop, the protesters lost heart and dispersed. The revolt was over in a fortnight.

Most East Anglian unrest was in Suffolk and Essex, passing Norfolk by, as did the Wars of the Roses in the fifteenth century. There was, however, one notable siege, that of Caister Castle, near Great Yarmouth. This moated, brick-built castle had been built by Sir John Fastolf – the inspiration for Shakespeare's Falstaff – from the ransom money paid for a French knight he had captured at Agincourt. From him it passed to John Paston of the great Norfolk mercantile and landowning family, but was claimed by John Mowbray, Duke of Norfolk, who set about taking it by force. After a gallant defence, the little garrison of thirty only succumbed when the Duke summoned reinforcements from King's Lynn; in any case, the Pastons recovered it eight years later.

A particular cause of unrest was the major landlords' enclosure of land for farming and sheep-rearing (see Chapter II) and this came to a head in the sixteenth century with a series of uprisings, by far the most serious of which was Kett's rebellion. Norfolk now created its own heroic, tragic legend; one that would have been remembered in ballads had it taken place among the Celts. The course of events is well known, but little about Robert Kett himself. A Norfolk hero to stand beside Nelson, there is no portrait of him and no written description. He was, however, a member of a robust Norfolk family, owning property around Wymondham and seemingly without a personal motive for rebellion. His is a story that must be told in some detail.

The unrest was not confined to Norfolk – there was also serious trouble in distant Devon – and the principal reason for it was changes in agricultural practice. In Norfolk, land-owners were enclosing arable fields, which their tenants farmed in individual strips, and common land, where all could graze their stock, and amalgamating them into large, managed farms, or sheep pastures to meet the growing demand for wool; indeed, when the rising began the rebels slaughtered sheep by the thousand in protest.

The spark that ignited Norfolk was, however, something different and a much older quarrel between neighbours. In Wymondham, there had long been acrimonious rivalry between the church authorities and the local townspeople and farmers, and this broke out in a furious quarrel over the ownership of the church building itself, which, over the past three centuries, had involved not only the King but the Pope. After the dissolution of the monasteries the town's monastic buildings were due for demolition, but the townspeople petitioned the King for permission to take possession of part of the monastic church adjoining their own. This was granted, but the royal agent, Sir John Flowerdew – a socially ambitious lawyer setting himself up as a country gentleman – continued the demolition with an eye to using the building materials himself. The result, in the summer of 1549, was a demonstration which turned into a riot and the leader of the protesters was Robert Kett.

In confronting Flowerdew, the demonstrators tore up the fences round his sheep walks and that long-simmering grievance against the enclosure of common land took fire again. So hot were the passions that Kett was inspired to show his solidarity with the crowd by tearing down his own fences. Thus, a popular leader was born: all that was needed for rebellion to spread. As messages of support reached him from distant parts of the county, Kett led his fellow-dissidents – mostly tradesmen and small farmers – to Norwich, the seat of power. Camped at Bowthorpe to the west of the city, Kett and his council drew up a list of grievances, mostly concerned with their freedom to work the land. Their camp was then visited by the High Sheriff of Norfolk, Sir Edmund Wyndham of Felbrigg, who commanded them to disperse in the King's name, formally accusing them of rebellion. He was rowdily ejected, as was the Mayor, who followed him. Two days later, when the rebels had moved to the west of the city, they were visited by Sir Roger Wodehouse of Kimberley who tried jolly persuasion, presenting them with two cart-loads of beer and one of food. But he misjudged their mood, was roughly handled, stripped and held captive.

Once more, Kett moved his horde again to Mousehold Heath on the hill overlooking Norwich from the east. There he set up a rudimentary administration, himself dispensing justice beneath a great tree known as 'The Oak of Reformation'. Having forwarded his demands to London and while awaiting reply, he relied upon Norwich for his supplies. Cowed by the presence of more than ten thousand potentially dangerous men on Mousehold, the city dared not close its gates and, in any case, many of the citizens sympathised with them. So an uneasy stalemate prevailed until the reply of the King's Council was delivered by York Herald, who reached Norwich from London on 21 July.

At Mousehold, the herald addressed Kett and his followers, declaring them rebels but offering them a royal pardon. Some of the crowd were relieved but Kett and his officers, convinced of the justice of their cause, did not consider themselves rebels and refused to surrender, or to disperse. So, accompanied by a few who had decided to accept the pardon, the herald returned to the city, which thereupon shut its gates and prepared to defend itself in the King's name.

Norwich was a fortified city. An area of two of the three miles of its perimeter was defended by walls and bastions twenty feet high and the remaining third by the river Wensum. The walls were in good repair but the city's total population of 13,000 could hardly raise enough able-bodied, armed men to defend them against a similar number of assailants. Also, the great Norman castle was ruinous and its earthworks offered little more than vantage-points on which to mount the few primitive cannon available.

Kett could not do without the resources of the city, however, so an attack was inevitable. After an ineffectual exchange of cannonballs, the assault began, Kett's men showing their zeal as they 'picked out the very arrows that were sticking in their bodies and gave them, all dripping with blood to the rebels . . . to fire again at the city'. Swimming the river to either side of the fortified Bishopsgate bridge, they outflanked it and were soon swarming through the narrow streets. Having occupied the city without further difficulty and having sent the herald on his way back to London, Kett left a small garrison to occupy strategic buildings and returned to Mousehold, taking some prominent citizens with him as hostages.

The herald reported to the King's Council a few days later and the Duke of Somerset, the Lord Protector, acted promptly. An expedition was hastily assembled under the Marquess of Northampton but, because of trouble elsewhere in the kingdom, it was a small one: some 1,500 men, including a contingent of Italian mercenaries. However, Northampton was accompanied by a number of peers and titled gentlemen, some from London and others who joined him on his march to Norwich in an increasingly colourful cavalcade.

Northampton halted a mile outside the city, which was nominally in the hands of the rebels, and sent a herald forward with a summons to surrender. The citizens, who were, in fact, overwhelmingly loyal to the King, immediately did so and, as Kett's men withdrew to their camp on Mousehold, the column entered. But that evening, while Northampton and his officers were dining, a party of the Italians went sightseeing and wandered beyond the walls towards Mousehold. There they were intercepted by rebel horsemen and their officer seized, taken up to the camp and hanged, probably not at Kett's orders and without his knowledge.

At once Northampton put his little army on a state of alert, concentrating his main force in the market place, from which it could be called to any threatened point on the perimeter. That night, Kett's artillery opened fire on the city with the usual lack of effect, but next morning the rebels assaulted the walls, helped by others hiding within the city. No quarter was given by either side and three hundred rebels were said to have been killed. There was an attempt by Northampton to arrange a truce and offer another pardon but this was again rejected as being inappropriate to loyal citizens, as the rebels saw themselves. On 1 August, another attack was made at the Bishopsbridge Gate, the rebels again swimming the river to outflank it and again bursting into the city. North of the cathedral a fierce fight began in a little square – now St Martin's-at-Palace Plain – where Northampton had parked his cannon. Both sides lost scores killed and wounded and among the former was the young courtier, Lord Sheffield. Several of Northampton's officers were captured, whereupon he withdrew not only from the battlefield but from the city, marching to Cambridge to await events and leaving the rebels victorious.

Kett now had time to consider his future strategy. He seems to have had no plans to overthrow the government in London but only to force it to initiate reforms and, for this, he needed more power in terms both of armed men and territory. Volunteers were not only joining him on Mousehold, however, bringing his army to perhaps 20,000, but they had also organised themselves in other parts of Norfolk, setting up camps at Watton, Hingham and at Castle Rising, from which they might be able to take King's Lynn. Nevertheless, at Great Yarmouth they failed, spurned by the citizens, who shut the town's gates in their faces and then sallied out to attack them. Meanwhile, the Norfolk gentry and their tenants were organising a counter-stroke, which persuaded some potential rebels that it would be prudent to await the outcome of the next inevitable move against Kett.

This came quickly. The King's Council was thoroughly alarmed: not only had the rebels trounced the Marquess of Northampton but the trouble in the west of England had increased; Exeter was under siege; and there was a risk of war with France. The trouble in Norfolk had to be extinguished quickly and decisively. The command of the punitive expedition was given to the efficient and ruthless Earl of Warwick and he was allocated a trained force believed to have numbered 6,000 infantry and 1,500 cavalry. The core of his force was to be a contingent of fourteen hundred *Landsknechts* – armoured German mercenaries – who would follow the main force to Norfolk as soon as they could be assembled.

So Warwick, collecting Northampton and the remains of his little army at Cambridge, reached Wymondham on 22 August. But even at this late stage, both sides were hoping that the issue might be settled without fighting. Another herald was sent to offer terms to Kett and again these were not even considered when the rebels were addressed as traitors. Once more the herald was heckled and jostled, and an archer in his escort shot dead a boy who had insulted him by baring his buttocks. Up to that moment Kett had probably been considering the terms and the possibility of negotiating face to face with Warwick under a flag of truce; he knew that he and the other leaders might be excluded from a general amnesty yet even that might have been negotiable. But the killing of the boy sparked an outburst of anger among his men and there was now no hope of calm consideration. A battle was inevitable.

Warwick's first objective was the city itself. Once that had been taken, his army would face the real battle against the rebels on the fortified heights of Mousehold Heath across the river.

However formidable in a scrimmage among hedgerows, Kett's men were neither disciplined nor trained for the defence of city walls. From within Norwich, the Mayor sent a message to Warwick, who had camped to the south-west of the city, telling him that his own men would open St Benedict's Gate and that another entrance to the walls, known as the Brazen Doors, could easily be forced. At first light, Warwick's artillery opened fire on St Stephen's Gate, shooting away the portcullis, and it was stormed by a phalanx led by the Marquess of Northampton, who had his reputation to recover, with a professional officer at his side to advise on tactics.

The western streets of the city were quickly overrun and, while rebels managed to hold out in the east, some were trapped and seized in the narrow streets; Warwick had forty-nine of them hanged immediately in the market place. Yet Kett's men performed one remarkable coup. Warwick's artillery train was following the infantry through St Benedict's Gate and its commander – like so many after him – was soon lost in the narrow, twisting lanes. Instead of turning right from St Benedict Street towards the market place, where they were to await further orders, they continued straight ahead towards the cathedral and along Bishopsgate Street, which, as they soon discovered, was still held by the rebels. So the guns were captured and set up on the far bank of the river, facing the city.

Kett thereupon launched a succession of counter-attacks. There was fierce fighting in the streets between the market place and the cathedral, particularly outside St Andrew's Hall. There Warwick himself, leading an attack down St Andrew's Street, was halted by rebel archers, but they in turn were taken in the rear by a company of arquebusiers, whose heavy muskets mounted on steadying props demonstrated the power of the new military technology.

Warwick's infantry were trained to assault fortifications and not in close-quarter fighting in alleys, where men with knives were often more lethal than armoured soldiers with pikes. After several day's fighting it seemed that Kett was beginning to prevail, attacking the city across the river wherever he found the perimeter more lightly defended, while keeping most of his army intact on Mousehold, threatening an overwhelming assault on the city. The Mayor and other leading citizens feared that Warwick might be bundled out of Norwich in the same way as Northampton and begged him to leave to spare the city from further destruction. His situation seemed precarious because he had not enough troops to storm the rebel camp of Mousehold but he decided to remain in the city for two reasons. One was that if he continued to hold it, the rebels should be forced to come down from the heights for want of supplies, and the other was that his fearsome German cavalry should by that time have arrived from London. Then, on 26 August, Warwick was disturbed during dinner by a fusillade of musket-shots: it was his 1,400 *Landsknechts* announcing their arrival with a *feu de joie*, ready for battle.

Each side awaited a move by the other, and, perhaps inevitably, it was the undisciplined rebels who first lost patience. Their leadership seems to have been divided, with Kett himself as the moderate, inhibited by loyalty to his followers, and some hot-heads (perhaps those who had hanged the Italian officer) advocating dramatic action. It may have been they who seized upon what was said to be a prophetic rhyme that was being circulated around the camp fires. This ran:

> The country gnoffes,
> Hob, Dick and Hick,
> With clubs and clouted shoon
> Shall fill the vale
> Of Dussindale
> With slaughtered bodies soon.

It seemed to go without saying that the slaughtered bodies would be those of Warwick's soldiers. So on that same night, they burned their camp on Mousehold and moved down to the low ground close to the river. It is not known exactly where Dussindale was but it is thought to have been to the north-east of the city. It was there that they set up their artillery behind hurriedly-dug earthworks and a stockade of sharpened stakes, while, in front, the prisoners – prominent citizens of Norwich and a few of Northampton's and Warwick's officers – were chained together as a shield.

Hearing of the move early on 27 August, Warwick acted quickly. Leaving most of his infantry to hold the city and as his reserve, he sallied from the St Martin's Gate with his cavalry and the *Landsknechts* and moved around the north of the city until he faced the rebels, massed behind the line of prisoners and their cannon. There was a final attempt to make terms and a small party of Norfolk gentlemen were sent forward under a flag of truce to offer pardon for all except the leaders of the rebellion. This was rejected and Kett's master-gunner fired a cannon, killing the royal standard-bearer.

So, disregarding both artillery and hostages, Warwick ordered the Germans to fire into the dense ranks. Then his cavalry charged. The rebels had faced nothing like this before and they broke. Panic seized them as the Germans advanced with heavy, armoured tread between each volley. Some fled for the open country while others, cut off by the cavalry, barricaded themselves behind their own baggage train. It was now up to Warwick whether to show mercy and he appeared to do so. Rebels making a last stand were offered an amnesty if they surrendered, and this they accepted. The battlefield fell quiet. It had been a hard-fought fight between peasants and trained soldiers, with the latter, although outnumbered two to one, prevailing. Eight of Warwick's Norfolk gentlemen had been killed – they were subsequently buried in St Peter Mancroft – together with about 250 of his soldiers. The losses among the rebels were never recorded but there may have been about 3,000 of their slaughtered bodies filling the vale of Dussindale.

The aftermath was as horrible as might be expected of that time. The rebels, who had rejected repeated offers of pardon, were guilty of treason under the law and the penalty prescribed was death. Nine of their leaders were hanged, drawn and quartered at the Oak of Reformation on Mousehold Heath, others died on gallows outside the Magdalen Gate and 300 were said to have been hanged in the market place.

Kett himself fled the battlefield and rode alone about ten miles to the village of Swannington, where he was recognised, seized and handed over to the authorities in Norwich. With his brother William, who had also been caught after the battle, he was sent to London and imprisoned in the Tower while awaiting trial. Both were condemned to death and taken back to Norfolk for execution. William Kett was hanged from the tall west tower of Wymondham Abbey, the church which had provided the spark that ignited the rebellion. In Norwich, Robert Kett was taken from his cell in the Guildhall to the castle and hanged in chains from the battlements.

Kett's Rebellion – the most serious of the civil disturbances in England during that turbulent year – helped bring about the fall of the Duke of Somerset's Protectorate and the Duke himself was executed three years later for plotting against his successor, the Earl of Warwick, who was himself to die on the scaffold. The rebellion, while it aroused mixed emotions in Norfolk at the time, became a tragic legend, reinforcing the East Anglians' suspicion of outside interference, whether by legislation, or military force. Kett became a Norfolk hero, an embodiment of resolute independence. The brief campaign he fought for what he saw as the rights of countrymen became *the* great battle in the county's history. Whatever battles had been fought against the earlier invaders, and whatever part Norfolk was to play in great conflicts, Kett's Rebellion was a brave, tragic little war and its story, handed down the generations, reflected the Norfolkman's idea of his own ideals and attitudes and the stand he was willing to make when they were challenged.

It was nearly a century before Norfolk passions were again so violently stirred. The conflict between King and Parliament found most of Norfolk supporting the latter while not wanting to become too closely involved with either. Rather, it was for mutual support that five East Anglian counties formed themselves into the Eastern Association with their administrative headquarters at Cambridge. Royalists within Norfolk were concentrated around the seats of several landowners, particularly that of Sir Hamon Le Strange at Hunstanton, close to the strategically important seaport of Lynn. But for all his hopes of remaining outside the Civil War already raging in the South Midlands, it was to East Anglia that Oliver Cromwell, the Huntingdonshire squire turned Parliamentary general, looked for recruits. It was the tough, independent-minded East Anglian countrymen who put on heavy leather riding-boots, breastplates and lobster-tailed helmets to become the formidable Ironsides.

Less than a year after the battle of Edgehill had opened the serious fighting, Norfolk found itself pitchforked into the war. Sir Hamon Le Strange, an archetypical cavalier with his coiffure, dashing mustachios and beard, and his frilly clothes, saw a chance to strike a decisive blow for the King. A strong character, Le Strange had persuaded the town council to declare for the royalist cause as he had been promised by the King that if Lynn were besieged an army would be sent overland, or by sea, to relieve it. He further persuaded them to shut the gates and hoist the royal standard. This they did.

Although the town was well-stocked with weaponry – including forty cannon – it stood little chance once the Parliamentarian majority of East Anglia mobilised and sent a warship to blockade the port. With customary ruthlessness, Cromwell decided on a quick decision by assault. The Old Town, outside the main defences, was quickly stormed and batteries sited there to bombard the walled town itself. Some eighty men were killed on either side by the cannonade, and when the defenders made a sortie to cut the dykes and flood the siege works, seven were captured and killed, their naked bodies displayed in view of the town. Finally, the Roundheads paraded before the walls with drums beating and colours flying. The formerly over-enthusiastic worthies of Lynn, who had allowed themselves to be fired by Sir Hamon's rhetoric, quickly surrendered.

Thereafter, Norfolk was secured for Parliament and East Anglia produced yet more recruits for the regularly-paid New Model Army, which finally prevailed. But before this, there was a counter-spasm of royalism throughout the country and, in Norfolk, it erupted in Norwich and resulted in what became known as 'The Great Blowe'.

Norwich, now the third city of England, had escaped the violence of civil war but by 1648 had, for all its citizens' sympathy for Parliament, become restive under Puritan restrictions. Frustrated by the banning of the city's favourite festivals, the citizens successfully petitioned the Mayor for the restoration of their traditional Christmas. As a result, he was arrested on the orders of Parliament, the people rioted and royalists took advantage of the disorder. Rioters rampaged through the city, breaking the windows of Puritans' houses and sometimes looting them. Surrounding the Parliamentarian Committee House, the crowd so frightened those within that someone fired a shot, killing a boy. Now the riot turned ugly, particularly when a troup of Parliamentarian cavalry rode up. There was a magazine of muskets, shot and gunpowder in the Committee House and as this was being looted, a powder-barrel was broken, a lighted lantern was dropped and the building exploded.

Both attackers and defenders were killed – the total was never known because of the number blown to pieces – and it was clearly an accident. Nevertheless, once the army had restored order, there came retribution and amongst evidence against the rioters was that one had been overheard saying, 'It were a good turn to goe and blow up the Committee House upon the Roundheads'. Eventually, twenty-four of them were briefly imprisoned and fined and eight hanged and regarded by their fellow-citizens not, perhaps, as martyrs but, as the register of the church of St Lawrence put it 'praetended mutineeres'.

That was the end of the counter-revolution such as it was in Norfolk, although there was far worse violence in Essex. Next year, the King was executed in Whitehall and the dour reign of the Commonwealth began. The Greate Blowe had been a dying kick of the Civil War and indeed was the last fighting on East Anglian soil (although its sea and sky were both to become theatres of war). The county was spared the violent folk-memories that linger elsewhere from this time, although an old house at Banningham is said to be haunted by the hoofbeats of a troop of Ironsides galloping through the village at night. What lasting effect the convulsion had on the county – other than re-affirming its distrust of an Establishment based upon a distant monarchy – was in the eclipse of the great royalist families: the Le Stranges never regained their former standing; the Pastons, already in decline, were extinct as a dynasty at the beginning of the next century. But the Wodehouses of Kimberley did survive to remain a force in East Anglian politics, when the rivalry was between Whigs and Tories rather than Roundheads and Cavaliers.

That same century, Norfolk heard the sound of distant guns as the Dutch – the enemy in two wars over trade and overseas expansion – were fought at sea off Lowestoft and Southwold and the traffic with the Low Countries was drastically interrupted. Later came the calls to arms as the county joined the rest of England to resist expected invasion by the French and then by the Germans.

As the first invaders had discovered, Norfolk is open to the sea, protected only by a few sandbanks and tidal currents. Defence on land could only be provided by the Army when it was summoned from London, or from other garrisons. Then, during the first spasm of fear at the possibility of invasion by the French, during what came to be called the Seven Years War in the middle of the eighteenth century, Norfolkmen were mobilised. It was the landowners who took the lead, particularly the Hon. George Townshend of Raynham, who, in 1757, steered the Militia Bill through Parliament, so founding a nationwide force of volunteers. In Norfolk, nearly a thousand men were recruited for two battalions. The Western Battalion was commanded by Townshend himself, the Eastern by Sir Armine Wodehouse of Kimberley, the family having recovered its political balance, and these two lieutenant-colonels, and the gentry who became their officers, devoted huge enthusiasm to recruiting and training.

The pioneer of military training was Townshend's cousin, William Windham of Felbrigg, who had made a hobby – but not a profession – of soldiering. As the former wrote – presumably of himself – in the militia's drill-book,

A worthy gentleman of Norfolk, though no regular bred soldier, nor an offspring of the parade, has endeavoured to prove how easily a healthy robust countryman or a resolute mechanic may be taught the use of arms; and how very attainable that degree of military knowledge is that will enable a country gentleman to command a platoon.

Military activities were not universally popular and Townshend's regular critic, the Earl of Leicester, mocked his efforts:

> The country rings around with loud alarms,
> And raw in field the rude Militia swarms;
> Mouths without hands maintained at vast expense,
> In peace a charge, in war of no defence.

In 1759, Windham took command of his battalion when Townshend was appointed one of Wolfe's three brigadiers in the expedition against Quebec, there, despite proving himself a troublesome subordinate, distinguishing himself and taking a command when Wolfe was killed at the capture of the city. The Norfolk militia never saw action but, under the command of Lord Orford, it was used as a strategic reserve and marched to Portsmouth to join the garrison of the principal naval base. Passing through London, they were reviewed by the King outside Kensington Palace, Horace Walpole noting of his cousin and his command,

> My Lord Orford, their Colonel, I hear, looked gloriously martial and genteel, and I believe it; his person and air have a noble wildness in them; the regimentals, too, are very becoming, scarlet faced with black, buff waistcoats and gold buttons. How knights of shires, who have never shot anything but woodcock, like this warfare, I don't know; but the towns through which they pass adore them.

Volunteer soldiers were again recruited for the wars with Revolutionary and Napoleonic France, a possibility that was greeted with a degree of over-excitement. In Reepham, for example, a parish meeting was called in 1798, 'respecting a sudden Invasion of the French &c. what was necessary and proper to be done on a Sudden Attack'. But this time there was more than the militia: infantry was to be provided by the volunteers, cavalry by the yeomanry, coastal defence by the 'sea fencibles'. Cadets of the Norwich Juvenile Regiment drilled with dummy muskets and tin bayonets and the more enthusiastic landowners raised their own little private armies.

Amongst the latter was Windham's son, also named William, who became Secretary at War – a Minister of State, as it were, to the Secretary of State for War. Young Windham argued against the formation of a large, part-time army of amateurs, instead urging the expansion of the regular army. But he did support the recruiting of local guerrillas in a scheme to be echoed in the establishment of the Home Guard in the Second World War. They, he suggested, would be made up of

> small divisions of two or three contiguous parishes . . . stationing an officer in each with a small deposit of arms and ammunition . . . to train those who should voluntarily offer themselves to such parts of military training as they would be alone capable of . . . It would never enter into my idea to introduce into bands of this sort any of the foppery of dress, or any distinctive dress at all; a riband, or even a handkerchief round the arm to distinguish them is all that would be necessary. Firing at a mark, learning, indeed, to fire at all, which (thanks to the Game Laws) few of our peasantry are acquainted with . . . firing from behind trees, retiring upon call and resuming a new station.

His plan, he said, 'draws no man from his home; it puts no man in a state of pitiful constraint; it stops no man in his business . . . It will produce that most important of all preparations, the preparation of the mind.' Thereupon Windham, with the help of an unemployed naval officer, set about training his own guerrillas at Felbrigg.

The danger of invasion sharply increased after the failure of the Peace of Amiens in 1802 and kept the country on the alert until Norfolk's Lord Nelson destroyed the enemy fleets at Trafalgar three years later. Brigadier John Moore – later to achieve fame in the Peninsular campaigns – toured East Anglian defences and, while he considered the Essex coast to be the most vulnerable, worried about Norfolk too. At Yarmouth he found the shore battery 'completely inadequate' and fit only to defend the port against 'the insults of privateers'.

The hero of the siege of Acre, Rear-Admiral Sir Sidney Smith, also gave his opinion that the Navy had no ships available to stop an invasion mounted from the Dutch coast.

This prompted Windham to stiffen the coastal defences, including those in the gap in the cliffs at Cromer, which was to be filled with a barricade of thorn-bushes strengthened by beached boats 'with sand thrown in to keep them steady'.

Gradually the ragbag of local volunteers were absorbed into larger infantry and cavalry formations, Windham himself taking command of the 4th (Cromer and District) Battalion of the Norfolk Volunteer Infantry. Sad at the standing down of the Felbrigg guerrillas, he consoled himself that, 'If I have this corps, I may make them exercise in the way I like, notwithstanding their red coats and feathers'. It was after Trafalgar in 1805 and the death of Pitt a little later, that Windham became Secretary of State for War. The emergency was over but he did much to improve national defence and, when he died in 1810, his epitaph in Felbrigg church declared that he had 'laboured to exalt the courage, to improve the comforts and ennoble the profession of a Soldier'.

Despite their understandable preoccupation with the defence of their county, Norfolk people were kept well-informed of foreign affairs by their newspapers, which carried reports from foreign capitals as well as London. The *Norfolk Chronicle*, in particular, described the mounting dangers and the measures taken to meet them, although the horrors of the French Revolution inspired sensationalism. In the premature report of the deaths of the King and Queen of France in 1792, it informed readers that the former had been 'beheaded before the eyes of the Queen, who was immediately hanged on the spot', and accompanied the more accurate account of the terrible death of the Princesse de Lamballe with a description of her 'most expressive sparkling black eyes' and her mind 'stored with the richest acquirements from the *belles lettres*'. Such lurid journalism had done much to promote recruitment and fire the martial fervour of its readers, amongst them the temporarily unemployed Captain Horatio Nelson at Burnham Thorpe.

When a victory was reported, church bells were rung. When news came that on 1 August 1798 the admiral from Burnham Thorpe had destroyed the French fleet in Aboukir Bay, the jollity knew no bounds. Many other Norfolkmen had taken part and celebrations spread throughout the county. In Norwich, windows were decorated at night with illuminated transparencies – one in a doctor's window showed a pile of cannonballs above the caption 'British pills effectively employed in the case of the French disease'; the militia fired 'three excellent vollies', and at a celebration ball the ladies wore bandeaux inscribed 'Nelson and Victory'. The coaches that carried the newspapers to the market towns flew flags and their guards fired their blunderbusses on arrival to attract attention to the news.

At Swaffham, Nelson's sister, Susannah Bolton, opened the ball and danced with the rector of Tittleshall, father of young Lieutenant Hoste, who had been promoted captain after the battle; a dance, named after the admiral's flagship, was 'called the *Vanguard*, or the breaking of the line', as her daughter noted. 'Mrs. Hoste's ribbands, which she had from London, were half Navy Blue and half red . . . Mrs. Micklethaite had had a very handsome cap from London inscribed in gold spangles, "The Hero of the Nile". '

Memories of what were to be called the Napoleonic Wars lingered long. In 1880, two old men met at a dinner party in a Norfolk country house. One of them, a squire named Jex-Blake, who hobbled on a wooden leg, heard the older man recall memories of the Battle of Waterloo, and how he had found and been able to help a young officer, whose leg had been smashed by a cannon-ball, but had never learned his name. When he finished his story, Jex-Blake told him, 'And I was the boy'.

Another memory lingered longer. During the years of danger from French invasion, it was recognised within the county that the most vulnerable stretch of coast was at Weybourne between Wells and Sheringham. 'This Waborne Hope, or Hoop . . . is the most dangerous place and most open to an enemy of any on the Norfolk coast', wrote a traveller in East Anglia, Samuel Pratt, in 1803,

> the shore is the boldest of any and transport-ships may approach so very near as almost to land an army without the assistance of flat-bottomed boats. It is an object worthy of consideration at the present time, when an

invasion from France is alternately threatened and attempted, whether it would not be proper to renew the fortification ... with batteries of heavy cannon to defend it ... In its defenceless situation, it seems to *invite* an enemy and to *court* an attack.

Defences had been built at the time of the Spanish Armada in 1588 and had been proposed, but not constructed, in 1793. Nor were they ready when Lord Nelson finally put an end to the danger in 1805. But the warning was not forgotten. During the First World War, a battery of coastal artillery was mounted there and a permanent range for anti-aircraft guns established. During the Second World War, Weybourne was defended with batteries of coastal and anti-aircraft guns and belts of concrete emplacements.

Victory in what was then known as the Great War with France produced the conditions under which imperial expansion could flourish. The British commanded the seas and were the principal traders on them; they had the ships and the seamen. The nation had been made more alert and efficient by the demands of war and, as about a tenth of the male population had been involved in some way – at sea in merchant ships, working in dockyards or in the local militia, if not in the active armed forces – there were men trained and accustomed to command and to obey.

The imperial ambition was primarily concerned with trade, although there was a strong impulse to spread civilisation, as it was seen in the home islands. Inevitably, there were clashes with rivals and those reluctant to be ruled. The colonial wars of the nineteenth century, culminating in the Boer War at its end, recruited soldiers from Norfolk, as memorials to squires' sons in parish churches and the names on the plinths of monuments on village greens testify.

It was in the summer of 1914 that the ordeals of the two world wars – one war, perhaps, with a twenty-year interval for the breeding of more fighting men – began with the shock of surprise. At the end of the century, old people still talked of that summer and some would recall the tennis parties which had been interrupted one August afternoon by telegrams recalling young men to their regiments.

At dawn on 3 November 1914, the old, recurrent nightmare of attack from the sea seemed to be coming true. Three German battlecruisers and three cruisers appeared near the Cross Sands lightship off Great Yarmouth and opened fire, waking the townspeople but causing no damage whatsoever. 'The early morning cannonade naturally caused a great sensation in Yarmouth', reported *The Times* next day. 'It began soon after 7 o'clock and continued for 20 minutes . . . The haze of an autumn dawn hung over the sea . . . All they could see was flash after flash on the horizon followed by the dropping of shells in the sea and the leaping of great cascades of water. The inhabitants were excited but not really alarmed.' The Germans also laid mines, which later sank a British submarine. Meanwhile, a light cruiser, the *Halcyon*, attacked them and they withdrew at speed. Soon after followed the much more serious bombardments of Yorkshire seaside towns and, early in the following year, British battlecruisers caught the raiders off the Dogger Bank and sank one of them.

Thereafter the Germans' High Seas Fleet kept its distance, but their airships and bombers ranged over East Anglia by night.

In the First World War, the Norfolk Regiment fielded twenty battalions and for the first time since the Danish invasions, Norfolk itself came under attack from the sea; also from the air. Aerial warfare did not take East Anglia wholly by surprise. Not only had balloon ascents been a popular sensation in eighteenth-century Norwich, but the development of the new medium had been followed in the newspapers. 'The French Government has removed to Tours, the only communication between it and Paris being by balloons', a Norfolk parson had noted in his journal for 1871. 'A German and French aeronaut fired at each other's balloons when at an immense height. Anything more desperately horrible it is hard to conceive.'

Spy mania had seized the country on the outbreak of war and so air-raids took on a highly personal motivation, as when the novelist Sir Rider Haggard believed a Zeppelin was attacking his daughter on her way home from a dance in

Bungay with her friend Dorothy Carr of Ditchingham Hall.
'What happened was the Zepp picked up the bright electric
lights which the chauffeur was forced by the police to turn on,'
he wrote in his diary.

> It lost them up our drive, where the trees and the ivy-covered house saved
> us, found them again on the road and followed them in the belief that it
> was one of their sympathisers leading them to a camp or works . . . since
> no German could be made to believe that on the very best night of a
> Zeppelin season, an Englishman would travel about at night with blazing
> electric lights except for some secret purpose. After the motor arrived at
> the Hall, the Zepp seems to have given it three minutes to get away, since
> Dorothy tells me she had just time to get to her bedroom when the bombs
> began to come . . . The terrific noise of these things and the uncertainty of
> where they are coming next is nerve-racking.

Norfolk suffered as much as the rest of England, five
thousand men being killed while fighting with the county
regiment alone, one-third of them on the Somme. Not all of the
dead were men, for one of the most famous of them was the
daughter of the vicar of Swardeston, Edith Cavell, executed by
the Germans in 1915 for helping British officers escape from
Brussels. Her last words were, 'I realise that patriotism is not
enough. I must have no hatred or bitterness towards anyone.'
Yet she was almost canonised as a martyr and recruiting for
the Army doubled in the nationwide thirst for vengeance.

In that same year, the county regiment – first raised to fight
the Monmouth rebellion in 1685, then becoming the 9th
Regiment of Foot – contributed to military mythology with a
legend to follow that of 'The Angels of Mons' of the preceding
year. This was the legend of 'The Vanished Battalion' of
Gallipoli: the 5th Norfolks. Poignance was added by the fact
that one of the lost companies had been recruited from royal
servants on the Sandringham estate. They had been led by the
King's land agent, Captain Frank Beck, and had been encouraged to join because the Territorial Army, to which they
belonged, had been founded in 1907 by the late King Edward
VII, the first sovereign to live at Sandringham House.

On 12th August, the battalion had been part of a brigade
attack on Turkish positions along the rocky spine of the

peninsula and they had last been seen charging into a burning wood. Later that afternoon, a witness had described a strange cloud rising above the battlefield, shaped like a memorial cross. The Norfolks, it was said, were never seen or heard of again; had there been something supernatural about their disappearance?

It was nearly eighty years before their story was put together and seen as a not untypical disaster of war that could represent many such on every front where the infantry fought. The attack had been led by Lieutenant-Colonel Horace Proctor-Beauchamp, who was smoking, waving his cane and shouting regimental exhortations, 'On, the Norfolks, on! Come on, my holy boys! Forward the hungry Ninth!' Local war cries were heard along the line of deployed companies as they moved forward, the hot sun flashing on their bayonets: 'Come on, Dereham, show them the point!' 'Forward the Lynns!' 'Come on, Yarmouth!' Turkish opposition was light at first and the attack surged forward, far ahead of any support, until it was in broken country of scrub and ravines and there the Turks were waiting.

One soldier, Private Tom Williamson, a former railwayman from Melton Constable, saw the line ahead of him wither under machine-gun fire and one group make for the shelter of a burning farmhouse: 'I saw a sergeant trying to rally his men around him. Many more already wounded and killed and those who could not walk were destroyed by the fire and others, who were actually inside the Turkish defences, were outnumbered and overpowered and, in any case were never heard of again.'

Not the entire battalion was lost but sixteen officers and 250 men were missing. After the war, a battlefield clearance party discovered a mass grave, and remains identifiable as those of one hundred and twenty-two men of the Norfolks; Colonel Proctor-Beauchamp's being identified by his silver regimental badges. It was clear that when the attack was broken among the Turkish defences, the Norfolks had fought on until all were killed and then the Turks had shot, or bayoneted, the wounded and those trying to surrender, except for a few saved by the intervention of a German officer. Among the dead was the King's land agent.

Afterwards, Private Williamson wrote a poem in memory of the young officer he had followed, as so many followed those they had seen as their natural leaders at home in Norfolk:

> My Officer was a vicar's son,
> He was lean and he was brave . . .
> As we advanced we were all as one
> And we knew the battle was on,
> With our bayonets fixed we all prayed
> As did the vicar's son,
> We knew the Turks had us covered well
> But on and on we ran,
> Then suddenly my Officer wounded fell
> Upon Gallipoli's scorching sand.
> And as I knelt to dress his wounds
> He told me to press on
> But I knew my Officer had heard death's sound
> As had many a mother's son,
> The Norfolk lads had played their part
> As indeed all soldiers can
> But through the fallen, and broken hearts,
> Peace must always stand.

While reading this and accounts of the battle and looking at photographs of the confident young officers and the trusting faces of their men, the boyish looks of one second-lieutenant seemed vaguely familiar. He had survived, I read, shot through the face and terribly disfigured. Then a memory, half a century old, came into focus of the bursar of one of my schools; a slight, quiet man, his face distorted and scarred by a wound suffered in the Great War; we knew no more. Now, looking at that photograph and reading his name, I realised that I had known a survivor of 'The Vanished Battalion'.

The youngest survivors of what they, too, knew as the Great War were still young enough to fight in the Second World War twenty years later; the older veterans joined the Home Guard, a revival of the militia and volunteers, which raised seventeen battalions. The coming of this war did not take Norfolk by surprise. All had watched the rise of Hitler across the North Sea and knew that Norfolk might again be directly threatened.

There was talk of German spies noting possible beaches for an invasion: why did that German *au pair* camping with the parson's family on Scolt Head Island go for such long early-morning swims and why did she hate having her photograph taken?

More than half-a-dozen military airfields already existed in Norfolk in 1939 and over the next five years, thanks to its proximity to the Continent and the availability of level ground, thirty more were constructed. At first, Wellington bombers took off on daylight raids against naval targets but the smart formations were intercepted by German fighters over the North Sea and cut to pieces. They were forced to make their raids by night, yet dangerous daylight attacks continued to be launched against German convoys off the far shore of the North Sea and these continued throughout the war.

It was the heavy bombers – particularly the Lancasters of Bomber Command and the Liberators and B17 Flying Fortresses of the United States Army Air Force – that so deeply marked Norfolk memories. The evening and morning air would pulsate with the sound of aero engines as the four-engined bombers lumbered off the runways, circled to gain height and joined the great procession, streaming across the coast towards Germany. Next day, village pubs would be crowded with young men in blue battledress or American khaki, the survivors, noisily drinking pints of weak beer in an attempt to dull the anticipation of the next operation or mission, as the British and Americans called their duties, and the probability that they would not survive the next three months, let alone the war.

Most of the courage and tragedy has now been forgotten except in the vaguest terms, and memorials are few. One of them, however, was set up near the airfield at Oulton half a century after the years it commemorates. The Royal Air Force officers, who flew bombers from there, lived at Blickling Hall, where, it is said, their senior officer slept in Anne Boleyn's bedroom. One day in June 1943, Wing-Commander King telephoned the station commander at Swanton Morley, Group Captain Spendlove, to ask if he would care to fly him on a short daylight operation to bomb the German airfield at Abbeville. Over the target, their bomber was hit, crashed in flames and both were killed. Such stories were commonplace in wartime Norfolk and the friends of the dead affected a nonchalance to avoid brooding upon those who had 'got the chop', or were likely to be the next.

Bomber Command had been joined in 1942 by the Americans of the 8th Air Force's 2nd Air Division and their airfields were spread across the south and east of the county as well as in Suffolk, Cambridgeshire and Lincolnshire. The social pattern they set in the surrounding villages was different from that of the RAF. both in style – for 'the Yanks' were exuberant, generous strangers – and often in the timing of their forays into the country pubs, for the Americans attacked by day, the British generally by night. The Liberators they flew would take off into the clear morning sky, most returning by dusk, some staggering across the sky, some burning in Norfolk fields, many failing to return; the number of young Americans of the 2nd Air Division killed in those years was 6,400.

One young British fighter pilot, Richard Hough, flying Typhoons on daylight operations from Ludham in the summer of 1943, later wrote,

When we were not on readiness, we would scrounge transport and go out in the evenings, avoiding Norwich which was horribly blitzed and packed full of airmen, British, Commonwealth and American, all on the booze, or after women. There were some nice pubs where we could swim in the Broads and lie in the last of the sun. The farmers were haymaking and the corn was ripening for a bumper harvest. American Fortresses would limp back in broken formation from a daylight raid. Early in the morning we had watched them gaining height, immaculately tidy and hopeful of success then, their contrails scoring the sky with white lines. Now their ordeal was over. Few of them, we could see, had four intact engines and their numbers were much reduced . . .

Once I went a hundred miles out to guide and talk back one of these savagely mauled Fortresses, flying close alongside. There were gaping wounds in the fuselage and both pilots and several gunners were dead. The navigator was flying her on two engines and the bomber was steadily losing height. I guided him over the coast and gave a course to his airfield but had to leave him because I was running out of fuel. I waved and wished him luck but never discovered if he made it.

Just as the air war began over East Anglian airfields, so it ended. At the beginning of March, 1945, as Germany collapsed under attack from east and west, the night fighters of the Luftwaffe staged a final fling. In Operation Gisela, 200 of them swooped on the great, black, four-engined aircraft of Bomber Command as they came in to land at their airfields, their crews exhausted after a night in the dangerous skies over the Continent. Twenty of them were shot down within sight of home, five of them over Norfolk.

The crews of the Royal Navy's motor torpedo-boats based at Great Yarmouth, where the dock area had been named HMS *Midge*, had something in common with the bomber crews, going to war by night and hoping to return at dawn. The difference was that their casualties were not nearly so high and they could anticipate eventual peace with more confidence. It was a brief experience of this form of warfare that gave me a moment of *déjà vu*, while snatching a short rest in the wardroom of an MTB, two hours out of Great Yarmouth, lying stopped and in wait for the enemy in the North Sea in the last months of the war. 'The gale had blown itself out and the wooden hull rocked on a gentle swell with timbers creaking,' I wrote afterwards:

> The night was dark and cold, but below deck, where it was light and warm, I had dozed briefly on a bunk. Some noise, unexpected amongst the soothing sounds and movement of the sea, had wakened me and, on opening my eyes, I saw frigates under sail. They were in a framed aquatint screwed to the bulkhead that showed British frigates blockading a French port during the Napoleonic wars. In that moment of waking, their image came together with what I could feel and hear and the realisation that the crews of those wooden ships would have lived with the same sensations. I felt a sudden kinship with them and an understanding of the continuity of the historical events that linked us. This was as real as it was romantic: Pitt and Churchill; Bonaparte and Hitler; Britain the beleaguered island. Then the noise that had wakened me began again. It was a harsh, metallic voice from the radio-telephone on the bridge above, 'Tartan to Bullfrog. Tartan to Bullfrog. Starshells and gunfire, bearing red zero five'. The odd call-signs, and now the thud of distant firing, brought me back to February, 1945 . . .

The MTBs based on Yarmouth – big, wooden boats, like miniature destroyers, slower than the German E-boats, but much more heavily armed – fought many sharp actions between there and Ijmuiden. But their greatest loss was accidental, when early in 1945 British and Canadian boats had established a forward base at Ostend. While the dock was crowded after a night operation, somebody threw a cigarette end over the side and it ignited high-octane fuel. In an eruption of flame, fuel tanks, torpedo warheads, depth-charges and ammunition exploded and twelve boats were destroyed with heavy loss of life. The disaster was kept secret at the time and, as an accident, has found no mention in naval history. I happen to remember because, but for one of those chances of war, I would have been there at the time.

In Norfolk, as everywhere else in England, Army camps proliferated together with artillery ranges, battle schools, supply depots and ammunition dumps. The Royal Norfolk Regiment (as it now was) itself raised seven active service battalions which suffered more than 2,000 killed in the five years. Five of these battalions were, indeed, lost: two in France and three in Singapore. During the German assault of 1940, when one battalion was almost destroyed near Dunkirk, ninety prisoners were summarily executed; yet a few escaped to help identify and track down the SS officer who had given the order, bringing him to trial and the hangman. The other battalion was trapped on the coast at St Valéry-en-Caux and forced to surrender, although one group managed to escape by boat, using shovels as paddles.

A more prolonged ordeal faced the three Territorial battalions, which had spent that summer defending the Norfolk coast, including the Weybourne Gap. Ordered to the Middle-East and trained for desert warfare, their convoy was diverted to Singapore when the Japanese attacked Malaya. Given a pamphlet about jungle warfare, they were landed just as the last defenders of Malaya retreated across the causeway and the Japanese assault on the supposedly impregnable base began. After a fortnight of confused fighting, Singapore surrendered but, as it did so, the Norfolks took two positive actions: the 4th Battalion packed its flag and its records into a coffin, which was inscribed with the name 'R. E. Cord' and buried with military honours (it was dug up intact after the war) and an official escape party was sent off disguised as fishermen (they finally reached India). Then the rest of the three battalions – some 3,000 strong – were marched to Changi prison.

The survivors of the brief fighting were still fit and well-fed, so set about organising themselves to face captivity. Then they were sent in groups to work on the railway being built by Allied prisoners of war through the jungle of Thailand, where they died by the hundreds from malnutrition, tropical disease and brutal treatment by their guards. Others were sent to work in Japan and many were drowned when the ship transporting them was torpedoed by an Allied submarine.

Curiously, nobody seems to know how many died in the next three and a half years. It is said that the battalions had been raised so quickly and moved so abruptly from camp to camp, then to South Africa and finally Singapore that accurate records were never completed, or, if they were, most were lost. The regimental headquarters in Norwich lists 438 as having been killed in the campaign, yet there are no statistics for those who died in hospitals at sea or in labour camps. There is a general belief amongst those who remember the time that only about thirty per cent of them came home. In Norfolk churches a stone cross-legged crusader is sometimes kept company by the carved names of these soldiers, and a few elderly men are pointed out by neighbours with the remark that they had 'had a bad time on the railway' and the meaning is clear.

Less horrifying but vivid memories of those tremendous years remain strong in Norfolk at the end of the century. In Great Yarmouth today, amidst the ice-cream and candy-floss, it is difficult to remember the war years when the Big Dipper stood derelict against the sky, and in sandbagged emplacements, the Bofors gun-crews huddled round their anti-aircraft guns, staring out to sea. Were those sea-stained motor torpedo-boats, with belts of point-five ammunition looped around their guns, really berthed alongside the fish quays?

For those who lived through them, those years have a dreamlike quality, or perhaps memories come in scraps, like disjointed clips of film. The occasional sight of a wartime newsreel, or a museum display, prompts the question, 'Was I *really* there?' Memoirs, written years later, also seem to have been seen through clouded glass. But it is the diaries written at the time – and these are rare – that catch the flavour and bring a twinge of recognition to those who were there.

In 1942, Sergeant-Major Leslie Paul was in the head-quarters of the 2nd Army, which was to land in Normandy on D-Day, based at Didlington Hall, south-west of Swaffham. He kept a diary, later published as a book, *Heron Lake*, which is more about his observations of birds in the woods and lakes around the house than about the war.

His diary (and others' memories) come alive when he suddenly refers to a Norfolk town in the context of history: 'I like Swaffham, it is spacious and clean and pleasant and in the square in the evenings the Gordons march and counter-march and play the retreat with their squealing pipe band.' Or:

Was at Cromer the other day, addressing some young subalterns and found time to swim and wander along the shore. In the blue sea air a mile or two out, the yellow-bellied Beaufighter training planes were practising machine-gunning a wreck . . . They rose up into the sky and hurled themselves angrily down at the wreck, lashing the sea with bullets. They were pterodactyls, clumsy and persistent and wooden with angry predatory angles . . . Children were walking the beach and it was a grim commentary upon the familiarity bred in all of us with weapons of death that they never once lifted their eyes to the planes but turned over stones, searching for fish and objects left by the receding tide.

Then: 'Visited Dereham church – as vast as a cathedral, I thought, yet more homely. There was a shy American soldier playing Bach on the organ and he told me he came from Massachusetts, where he earned his living as an organist, and wherever he goes in England he gets permission to play the local organ in his spare time.'

Finally the war itself:

During the night, the hut trembled and shook and the window frames rattled . . . 'Did yer hear that? Bleeding Jerry!' . . . 'It's miles away,' I said. 'Probably Norwich or King's Lynn' . . . 'Bleeding Jerry . . . I've got a girl in King's Lynn and another in Norwich. What the hell does he think he's doing?' He sat still listening to it, but I rolled over and went to sleep. It was Norwich ... Norwich has few troops in it, some aircraft and clothing factories, lots of nice people, poor devils, and absolutely no defences.

In 1959 the Royal Norfolks were amalgamated with the Suffolks to form the 1st East Anglian Regiment and this in turn became the Royal Anglian Regiment. In such guises, they fought in the little colonial wars brought about by the controlled disintegration of the British Empire. They joined allies in NATO facing the threat from the Soviet Union and its empire on the plains of central Europe. If a reminder of the danger were needed, the huge battle-training area north of Thetford, which had been cleared for the purpose in 1942 and had left the villages of Stanford, West Tofts and Tottington as empty as their neighbours, Langford, Sturston and Buckenham, which had been deserted in the Middle Ages, was still being used by the Army; while they did so, Norfolk skies again howled with the aero-engines of the British and American air forces. While the United States Air Force was again based on East Anglian airfields, the sight of the needle-nosed fighters, or stubby ground-attack aircraft flying to their off-shore ranges became familiar as they trained for their part in the punitive attacks on Libya in 1986 and later the Gulf War of 1991 against the Iraqi dictator.

The threat from the Soviet Union has been replaced by a less discernible but even more disturbing sense of danger from a world where the established order seems to be breaking apart. Despite the political and economic alliances with old enemies on the Continent and cuts in defence expenditure, Norfolk retains its strategic importance as an enormous natural airfield. There will be more sombre memories for future generations, it seems probable.

II
Land

Seen from the air, Norfolk is painted in shades of green and
brown. These are rich, healthy colours, so different from the
arid yellows, vivid emerald or ash grey of the world's
deserts, swamps and mountains. The colouring is symbolic of
prosperity for the riches of Norfolk have always been in its
soil. There have been no minerals to mine (beyond a little
ginger-coloured carrstone and chalk in the west) and no rushing
rivers to harness for the creation of power greater than that
of the watermill. Yet much of its soil is rich, and the growing
of crops and the grazing of sheep and cattle were the
foundation of its wealth and that of the powerful families
who farmed its great estates and built its mansions. This is
the desirable land for which the invaders crossed the sea and
which, once they themselves became its inhabitants, they
fought to defend.

The land was laid down by seas and glaciers. Yet it has a
variety that shows both in its differing landscapes and in
farmers' account books. The underlying rock or shingle floor
of Norfolk is tilted slightly to the south-east with the highest
land in the north-west. It was the Ice Age, between one and
two hundred thousand years ago, that made Norfolk what it
is. Before that time, as scientists have discovered, it was like
Siberia, a vast tract of pine and birch. When the ice melted, it
left deposits of clay, gravel, loam and sand and in this grew the
broad-leaved trees that still survive, notably oaks in the heavy
clay of the centre and south-east, sometimes 250 metres deep.
Elsewhere, the glaciers left a variety of land: the rich peat of the
east and west (the Broads, which were originally peat
workings, and the Fens); the light, sandy soil of the north-east;
the chalk downs of the north-west; and, in the west and

south-west, the silt at the head of the Wash; the stony outcrops of the western escarpment and the sandy heaths of Breckland.

'Norfolk is compounded and sorted of soyles apt for grayne and sheepe and of soyles apt for woode and pasture', it was said in the sixteenth century, and so it remains. The men who first inhabited the fringes of the great forests, along the sea shore, the river banks and the edges of the water-logged Fens, grew crops, kept cattle and hunted wildfowl. As new settlers arrived from across the North Sea, more woodland was cleared. Under the Romans, land was farmed in estates only to be abandoned and farmed again between the devastation of Anglo-Saxon raids and eventual settlement that followed the collapse of the Roman Empire.

The greatest change was after the Norman invasions of 1066, when an elaborate system of tenancies was established under those Norman barons and bishops who had been rewarded with land, and the monarch himself, who was the largest landowner in the county. The Domesday Book shows that farming became most intensive in the east, particularly with sheep grazing on the coastal levels, where salt was also produced, as it was on the shores of the Wash.

By the time that the Middle Ages gave way to the Tudors in the sixteenth century, farming in Norfolk had further evolved. Now it was on the light land of the north and west that vast flocks of sheep grazed, the lord of the manor having the right to grazing on his tenants' land while it was lying fallow between the harvest and the next sowing. Meanwhile, the heavy clay-country of the centre and south-east was best suited to cattle, while the land on the verge of the undrained Fens and Broads produced rich cereal crops and hay.

Already there were the makings of a rural underclass: the landless labourers, constantly on the verge of destitution were, at times of poor harvests, driven to poaching to avoid starvation. Above them were the smallholders, who needed to farm between ten and fifty acres to support a family; then came the tenant and yeoman farmers, the gentry and the land-owners. The elaborate Norman system of owners' and tenants' rights had led to abuses, as greedy farmers tried to convert seasonal rights into permanent rights with use of the land for grazing between harvest and sowing, usually by fencing it within their own territory. This was one of the injustices that spurred Kett's Rebellion.

Such enclosing of land began in the Middle Ages and continued for centuries. This involved the landlord calling in tenancies of the strips of field worked by individuals and reorganising the strips into enclosed fields, which he either kept or let. So, gradually the economics of scale began to eclipse the smaller farms.

The Pastons, medieval rural gentry of exceptional drive and ability – like most of the Norfolk aristocracy, they began as successful squires rather than relations of royalty, or descendants of Norman nobility – burst from the confines of the coastal village that bears their name to become the dominant family in the county for more than two centuries. Their progress from hard-working farmers – the great thatched barn at Paston, still stands, recalling the scale of the riches they drew from their land – to East Anglian grandees, was powered by ambition and their understanding of the law. Their struggles through the fifteenth century, not only legal but sometimes military, were described in the marvellous cache of papers, known as the Paston Letters, discovered five centuries later. In the Norfolk historian Wyndham Ketton-Cremer's words, these told of

> the fights and wrangles and disputes; the sieges of Gresham, Hellesdon and Caister; the bullying by great territorial magnates; the appeals to Kings and Bishops; the anxiety and suspicion and alarm; the painful gathering of rents and dues, the carefully arranged marriages, the litigation and the petty bargaining; the shrewd capable, calculating wives, seeing to affairs in Norfolk, while their husbands or their sons waited at Court, hoping for a chance word from the King. And, as the final result, a great family and a great name; power and titles, broad lands and luxurious houses.

In these letters, the Pastons of the fifteenth century stand out in high relief, the whole being an extraordinary echo of the survival of family life in those violent times, notably during the Wars of the Roses and those reign of King Richard III. Then, the redoubtable Margaret Paston could write to her husband John in London asking him to send her crossbows because the ceilings of their house were so low that long-bows could not be fired from its windows. This was no imaginary threat for the Pastons' manor at Gresham had been stormed by a thousand men, sent by Lord Moleyns, equipped with the latest military technology, 'arrayed in manner of war, with cuirasses, briganders, jacks, sallets, glaives, bows, arrows, pavises, guns, pans with fire burning therein, long cromes to drawn down houses, ladders, picks with which they mined the walls and long trees with which they broke up gates and doors'.

Most memorable then, but most thoroughly forgotten now, was their most luxurious house, Oxnead Hall. This was built by Clement Paston, a soldier, a sailor and courtier, to replace their original home, isolated on the coast at Paston, and the castle at Caister they had inherited from Sir John Fastolf. In striking contrast to both the windswept farmstead and the moated keep, Oxnead seemed to loll luxuriantly on its terraces, among statues, fountains, follies and ornamental trees. Clement was succeeded by his nephew Sir William Paston, the founder of the Paston School at North Walsham, which was to count Nelson amongst its pupils, and, in 1632, the house, together with the family's vast estates, passed to another William Paston, widely travelled and a man of taste with, of course, the money to indulge it. It was he who transformed Oxnead into a gigantic cabinet of curiosities. Built above the river Bure with formal gardens descending by terraces to the water, it was the embodiment of Jacobean taste, so sumptuous in high summer that Paston's chaplain wrote of winter,

> When Hills, and valleys, wrap't in sheets of Snow,
> Did pennance for their summer luxury.

Oxnead flowered in the decade before the Pastons took the royalist side in the Civil War, fatally damaging their interests in Parliamentary East Anglia. Sir William survived the Civil War and lived to welcome the Restoration and entertain King Charles II at the house. But, like a great oak that has come to the end of its span, the family withered and its vitality was gone by the time of his grandson.

Extravagance had not been balanced by strength of character and when the last William Paston died in 1732, his three sons were already dead, and so the family itself petered out; finally, the great house itself was sold and its contents dispersed. Some of the stone embellishments have been identified at Blickling but the only real reminder of what it was like is a painting by an unknown artist, *The Treasures of Oxnead*. This pile of Venetian glass, English silver, Florentine musical instruments, assorted objects of *vertu*, a cornucopia of fruit and a lobster watched over by a Negro page and his pet monkey is a timeless depiction of unabashed luxury. The treasures were sold – 'the crystall tankard with a cristall cover, set in a silver and gilt frame with two handles, a flying horse on top', the 'white agat dish in fashion of a heart with a white rose in it', the 'mother of pearl shell, the fashion of a boat, standing upon a silver and gilt foote upheld with two anchors, with two spoones in it, one christall and one amber'- such beautiful, impractical knick-knacks, themselves symbolising what the family itself had become. Where are they now?

The estate itself was sold to Admiral Anson, who had just returned from his voyage round the world, rich with Spanish gold, but who had no interest in the splendour of Oxnead, regarding the purchase purely as an investment.

Oxnead was demolished except for its kitchen wing, itself the size of a substantial manor house, and the terraces became overgrown. It had one particularly suitable owner, a young man of means who bred otters, and whose wife was an amateur jeweller. It was recently bought by a successful photographer, who has spared no expense in restoring the famous terraced gardens, planting a handsomely authentic parterre, rebuilding an octagonal tower on the river bank, but introducing the whiff of a Tudor theme park.

As Oxnead fell, other great houses arose. In the middle years of the eighteenth century, architects were conjuring up designs for a score of magnificent mansions and many lesser but substantial houses to be supported by the produce of their surrounding estates. With the Stuarts came the first serious attempt to drain the potentially rich fens and salt-marshes with the help of Dutch engineers. Since the rich, reclaimed land had never been farmed, it could be bought by investors and it became the foundation of agricultural fortunes. Since Roman times, the edges of the great estuary that emptied into the Wash had been drained and reclaimed by farmers, who had known of the richness of the silt. But now new dykes drained the fens and rivers carried away the water from the wide marshlands, leaving vast, flat, fertile fields. The peat fens were also drained but this caused the level of the land to fall so that windmills had to be used to pump water from the dykes into the rivers, which now flowed above the level of the fields. In the east of the county, peat had been cut for fuel throughout the Middle Ages – its use is thought to have been introduced by Danish settlers who had burned peat for centuries in Denmark – and these workings having flooded, they became shallow lakes known as the Broads, which were valuable for fishing and wildfowling. Around the coast the draining of the salt-marshes of the north-west began in the seventeenth century but this was curtailed by shortage of labour during the Civil War.

There, and on higher ground, the raising of livestock became immensely profitable: generally, sheep in the west and cattle in the east. Wool had made many farmers rich and the tangible signs of this are the great churches of the grazing-lands and the mansions of the landowners.

So Norfolk became a county of big farms, prosperous estates and noble mansions. An eighteenth-century writer on agriculture wrote of this landscape:

I shall only observe that the vast improvements, which have been made in Norfolk by converting boundless heaths, sheepwalks and warrens into well-cultivated districts, by enclosing and marling, are such as were never yet made by small farmers. Great farmers have converted in this county three, or four hundred thousand acres of waste in to gardens ... Little farmers have never, in any county that I am acquainted with, produced equal effects ... The Norfolk farmers are famous for their great improvements, the excellency of their management and the hospitable manner in which they live and receive their friends and all strangers that visit the county.

Innovation was abroad. In 1771, the agriculturalist Arthur Young wrote in his *Annals of Agriculture* that there were now seven pillars of improved farming in the county: the enclosure of open fields and commons; the rotation of crops; the use of marl to reduce acidity in the soil; the growing of turnips as winter feed for cattle and to clear the land through cultivation; the growing of clover; long leases for tenant farmers; finally, bigger farms. He did not, however, mention the importance of improved drainage, or the improvement in livestock by selective breeding. Innovation was followed by mechanisation. In 1805, the year of Trafalgar, the only machinery that was likely to appear on a farm inventory was the plough. Half a century later, there would also be threshing machines, chaff-cutters, dressing machines, oil-cake crushers and the rest.

The credit for this combination of efficiency and munificence has been concentrated upon Thomas 'Coke of Norfolk' at Holkham and 'Turnip' Townshend of Raynham. They were the most famous, but the true innovators were the farmers of the county's north-east, who often took their ideas from the Low Countries across the North Sea. Yet it was Coke with his annual sheep-shearings from the 1770s to the 1820s, which became the forerunner of the county agricultural shows, who was the master of public relations as much as the technology of farming. It was his interest in farming as a way to great fortunes that encouraged the boom that reached its peak at the end of the first half of the nineteenth century.

Yet the lot of the landless labourer – usually hired by the day, so unemployed and unpaid in bad weather – had not improved. When Captain Horatio Nelson was living at Burnham Thorpe on half-pay and farming his father's glebe land, he was appalled by their conditions and took the brave step of writing about it to his friend the Duke of Clarence (the future King William IV) at a time when the government was hyper-sensitive to any opinion that might be considered radical and subversive.

In this long letter, written in December 1792, he blames the
success of the revolutionary movement in England to this rural
poverty.

> That the poor labourer should have been seduced by promises and hopes
> of better times, your Royal Highness will not wonder at when I assure
> you that they are really in want of everything to make life comfortable.
> Parts of their wants, perhaps, were unavoidable from the dearness of
> every article of life; but much has arose from the neglect of the country
> gentlemen.

He then set out a table of earnings and expenditure on
essentials, showing that, as he wrote, 'Not quite twopence a
day for each person; and to drink nothing but water, for beer
our labourers never taste, unless they are tempted, which is too
often the case, to go to the Alehouse.' The contrast between
their damp, earth-floored cottages and the marble halls of the
super-farmers for whom they toiled could hardly have been
greater.

Grazing rights on common land were revoked and these
additional acres also converted into hedged fields. There were
two main consequences: one bad; one good. The bad was that
the peasant became a labourer, dependent upon his master's
wages and bounty instead of working to feed himself and his
family; here the foundations for rural poverty, which persisted
into the twentieth century, were laid. The good was that the
larger farms became far more efficient, crop yields increased
and the pioneering farmers of the eighteenth century could
spread their reforms over much wider areas.

While the landowners lived in splendour, the farm workers
who had made this possible lived either in near-destitution or
under threat of it. At the time of Coke's death, about an eighth
of Norfolk countrymen were unemployed and there were
virtually no provisions for the alleviation of their distress,
except local charity and a few 'workhouses' to give them
shelter. At the end of the war with France, grain prices had
fallen but so had agricultural wages. In 1816, food was scarce
and riots broke out in the west of the county; this was put
down ruthlessly, fifteen rioters being sentenced to death and
two of them finally hanged. Technology was beginning to

make itself felt as the industrial revolution reached the farms. The new threshing machines, which deprived labourers of their traditional winter employment, were particularly unpopular; many were smashed or burned during the riots which broke out across the county in 1830. To keep grain prices at an economic level the Corn Law was passed, prohibiting its import until British prices had risen; so helping the farmers but not farm workers.

Yet efficiency and prosperity increased and reached a peak during the middle years of the nineteenth century. The day of the big farms was still to come because less than two per cent of Norfolk farms were of more than 1,000 acres. In 1850, more than half were of less than 100 acres and not much more than a quarter were between 200 and 300 acres. At that time arable land was almost equally devoted to grain crops and root or temporary pasture. Wheat was the most profitable grain crop but Norfolk soil was better suited to barley, for which the county became famous. Dairy cattle were not of importance but large flocks of sheep were kept on the light soil of West Norfolk.

The village itself was a balanced community, which seems enviable today. Taking a typical village, buried deep in the countryside, the agricultural historian Dr Susanna Wade Martins has analysed the employment structure of Tittleshall, south of Fakenham.

> Its population numbered 615 in 1851, when it supported a grocer, a shoemaker, a baker, a draper and several butchers. There were also bricklayers and makers, thatchers, blacksmiths, wheelwrights, hurdle-makers and fishermen. Just over half the working population were agricultural labourers . . . This pattern was repeated in nearly every mid-19th century Norfolk village.

After the boom came the depression and it was brought about by several factors, one being the imports of cheap grain from the American mid-west. With the decline in farming, combined with a succession of bad harvests in the second half of the century, employment and wages fell and farm workers, defending their meagre livelihoods, formed agricultural trade unions.

By 1880 the shape of Norfolk farming had changed and the day of the great estates, supported by the rents of tenant farmers, had arrived. Some, of course, belonged to the old landowners, who owned all the estates with more than 15,000 acres: Lord Leicester of Holkham held 43,000 acres split into more than eighty farms, Coke himself working only about a thousand acres; the neighbouring Lords Townshend and Walpole each owned between 15,000 and 18,000 acres at Raynham and Houghton respectively. It was the middling estates that predominated and, as the slump in agriculture impoverished small farmers – rents on the Holkham estate halved over the next thirty years – their richer neighbours bought their land. So now more than half of the county was owned by those with more than 1,000 acres.

Yet, a century after Nelson's report, the lot of the farm worker had not improved. Now he found a champion in Rider Haggard, the farmer-novelist of Ditchingham, who deplored that this life of hard work and hardship should all too often end in the workhouse. Haggard had stood for Parliament and almost won East Norfolk for the Conservatives but they were probably relieved that he did not win because of the surprisingly radical ideas he had proposed to solve the problem of rural poverty. One was, as he wrote, 'The case of a deserving labouring man ought not to be beyond the reach of some system of insurance' and he must have had in mind such national insurance as was introduced by a Labour Government half a century later. He recommended the creation of a new class of smallholder, whose land would have been compulsorily purchased, initially from the Church of England's estates.

None of his ideas for reform was put into practice at the time; conditions had only marginally improved before wages were substantially increased after the Second World War, shortly before the labourer himself was largely replaced by machines. No wonder, then, that the Victorian and Edwardian farm workers, who tended livestock for a prosperous farmer but were rarely able to feed their own children with meat, took to poaching. So long as this was dictated by need, there was

48

little criticism in the villages; on the contrary, there was a certain admiration for an experienced poacher, who snared, or netted the squire's rabbits.

The depression lasted for almost half a century, until it was relieved by the sudden outbreak of war with Germany in 1914. Then the blockade of the British Isles by submarines made home-grown food vital for survival: the Government intervened to encourage farming and pay its workers a more realistic wage. The wartime boom was followed by another depression, aggravated by death-duties which brought about the sale of many estates; a quarter of English farmland changed hands over four years. This upheaval led to many tenant farmers buying the land they worked. Again, East Anglian farmers faced competition from abroad, notably from Canadian wheat, New Zealand lamb and Argentinian beef. New crops were introduced, particularly vegetables, fruit, flax and sugar beet. This root crop, introduced by the Dutch, as so many practical ideas had been in the past, became hugely successful. In parallel, the great flocks of sheep dwindled in the face of foreign competition but, for the first time, Norfolk turned to dairy-farming and, within 20 years, had become an important milk-producing region. Yet still the overall decline continued with land selling for less than £10 an acre and commanding less than ten shillings in annual rent. Again, the industry was saved by war in 1939 and wages were once more raised.

In 1940, German tanks were rolling across the plains of France as the first combine-harvesters began to grind across the fields of Norfolk, both harbingers of the new technology. When swords were finally beaten into plough shares five years later, the day of the farm labourer was finally done with agriculture employing more men and women in its related processing and canning plants than in its fields. One farm of 500 acres at Nelson's village of Burnham Thorpe employed twenty labourers at the outbreak of the First World War; by 1980, when the acreage had been increased, there were nine, and in 1994, three; another farm of 1,000 acres, which was also employing three men at the end of the twentieth century, had given work to thirty labourers forty years earlier. Social life in the country declined with employment – in forty years following the Second World War, the 250 families living on the Sennowe estate were reduced to fifty. Gone, too, was the lovely landscape of farmland: first, the work-horses were declared redundant; then the hedgerows were uprooted by the mile as unproductive; across the new prairies, the agricultural machines crawled like tanks. With the disappearance of the horse and the replacement of the farm labourer by the semi-technician driving a combine-harvester, the post-war farms would have been almost unrecognisable to Rider Haggard's generation.

If the election of a Labour Government in 1945 seemed to promise the future security of the small farmer, this was not the case. Their legislation of 1948 and 1976 was designed to strengthen the tenant farmer's security by enabling him to pass his lease on to his children, and then grandchildren, but it had the opposite effect. Landowners saw that not only would they be unable to get rid of the bad farmers amongst their tenants, but that their land was slipping from their estates, and they imagined that the right of outright purchase by tenants might follow. So, as soon as it became legally possible, landowners took leased farms back and either installed managers, or introduced tenants willing to farm on a profit-sharing basis without their heirs having rights of inheritance.

The landowners themselves were changing. Farms were being bought by big city-based companies – foreign as well as British – both for their own commercial production and as long-term investment. City financiers, who had never seen mud on their shoes, bought farms to set against taxation, or even as a new hobby for their weekends in the country. By the end of the century, the most important landlords in Norfolk were the administrators of pension funds and insurance companies – including the Norwich Union – and the manager in his Range Rover had replaced the farmer on his pony.

The small farms of the mid-nineteenth century, and even some of the big estates, had been replaced by conglomerates a century later. Between the 1960s and the 1980s, the number of small farms of less than 100 acres more than halved and almost all the buying and selling by farmers in market towns had ceased.

One consequence of the intrusion of Big Business into the countryside was that the land, as an investment, had to bring the maximum returns and that meant the intensive use only made possible by drenching the fields with chemical fertilisers. Small wonder, then, that Norfolk came to have one of the highest rates of poisonous nitrates in its drinking water. This was often spread by vast machines to which the surviving hedgerows were obstacles that must be removed, whatever the risk of dry topsoil blowing or washing away, let alone the destruction to the nesting-places of wild birds.

Britain's entry into the European economic system brought further changes. Under the European Economic Community policy, the price of wheat more than tripled, while the production of barley – the traditional Norfolk crop – fell, and the acreage devoted to sugar beet increased by a quarter. The numbers of cattle fell dramatically, but pigs increased as did ducks and turkeys, the latter being mass-produced in the largest industrial concern of its type in Europe by the turkey farmer Bernard Matthews, who put his broad Norfolk accent to good use in television advertising. However, the traditional landscape of farmyard and meadow has now largely gone and has often been replaced by dreary compounds of single-storey huts, where livestock is kept living indoors, often in small pens, fed and watered automatically, living their short lives in electric light.

With over-production brought about by subsidised industrial farming, much land has been declared redundant and farmers are paid to 'set aside' fields, or encouraged to use land for purposes other than farming. Fields which had once borne crops, or fed sheep and cattle, have become caravan sites, golf courses and theme parks. Around towns and villages there is constant pressure from developers anxious to build on agricultural land, not practical houses for the indigenous population but, all too often, 'executive homes' for commuters, or supermarkets that undercut the remaining village shops.

Even the prosperous and well-administered Holkham estate was guilty of pressing for planning permission for the former outside the hitherto unspoiled village of Burnham Market.

Farming and its by-products – beer, leather, mustard, food canning – made fortunes and established dynasties. The great houses the first medieval wool magnates built have mostly been demolished or rebuilt, but their soaring churches remain as symbols of thanksgiving to God and of worldly riches to men. The wealth of the landowners grew with the increase of rents which accompanied agricultural progress, and this led to the building of palaces like Houghton, Holkham, Didlington, Kimberley, Gunton and many more. Landowners became politicians, patrons of the arts, or just rich men giving employment to those catering for whatever their tastes happened to be. The paladins of them all were, after the Pastons of Oxnead, the Walpoles of Houghton and Wolterton, the Townshends of Raynham and, of course, the Cokes of Holkham. For them, land represented wealth and power and one purpose of the great parks and avenues that they laid out around their mansions was to demonstrate that and to make the point that they had land to spare for the creation of picturesque landscapes, or for field sports.

The great landowners of the span of time reaching from the arrival of the Hanoverian monarchs early in the eighteenth century, through to the reforms and innovations of the first half of the nineteenth, were men of parts. The greatest of the Walpoles, Robert (1676–1745), was one of less than half a dozen of the most significant politicians on the Westminster stage in that century, notably as prime minister for a total of twenty-one years between 1715 and 1742. As early as 1712, Daniel Defoe could joke when visiting King's Lynn, 'I found myself out of His Majesty's Dominions and in the capital city of the territories of King Walpole'. He finally retired to Norfolk to live in splendour as the Earl of Orford.

In Norfolk, Walpole left Houghton Hall as his monument. Built in the 1730s to designs by the architects Colen Campbell (also the architect of Stourhead in Wiltshire) and Thomas Ripley (also the architect of the Admiralty in Whitehall), the interior was by William Kent (the designer of the interior of Spencer House, here on his first major commission), and it reached the height of Georgian taste and grandeur with its disciplined marble and riotous plasterwork; the four corner turrets were ordered by Sir Robert himself. Houghton was ready for Walpole's retirement from public life, although he was to survive only three more years. The house and estate survive and can be seen as the whole was intended: the white peacocks in the garden and the white deer in the park are an integral part of the composition.

A neighbouring landowner, Charles Townshend (1674–1738), was also one of the great statesmen of the eighteenth century. But he is remembered in Norfolk less for his direction of British foreign policy than for pioneering the use of root crops for winter cattle-feed to avoid the traditional slaughter of livestock each autumn, which won him the nickname 'Turnip'. Like Walpole, his political rival, he spent his final years – in his case, the eight following his retirement from politics – at his country seat. Raynham Hall, near Fakenham, had been built early in the seventeenth century to a design sometimes attributed to Inigo Jones. Although a century older than Houghton and smaller, it displayed equal but different elegance with its red brick and Dutch gables, particularly when seen across its park from the road to the east of the house.

He is remembered as 'Townshend of Norfolk' for his experiments with crops and the rotation that became known as 'The Norfolk System', which predated more celebrated innovations by more than half a century. A striking man by all accounts – big, burly and short-tempered – his fame relies on his nickname rather than the achievements that won it.

Perhaps the greatest, and certainly the most famous of the great houses, was Holkham, built on a sandy coastal site where once, it was said, two rabbits could be seen fighting for one blade of grass. This was the creation of two remarkable men both named Thomas Coke and this remained their family's home from the middle years of the eighteenth century. The first Thomas Coke (1697–1776) had inherited the Holkham estate at the age of ten. Before he was twenty he had embarked on the Grand Tour, spending six years in Italy, acquiring a taste of Italian art and bringing back to Norfolk crates of pictures and statuary, packed, it is said, in ilex fronds, from which, tradition has it, grew the groves of evergreen oak that still decorate the park.

The creation of Holkham Hall and its micro-world of parkland, vista, lake and follies was inspired by the building of Sir Robert Walpole's mansion at Houghton. The first designs were drawn around 1725 and the foundation stone laid in 1734 on what had been a dreary, undulating stretch of heath along the coast. Coke dammed a stream to form a lake, planted broad-leaved trees over the low chalk downs around it and in the centre – and the vortex of the architect's artfully arranged vistas – he built his massive Palladian mansion.

Perhaps his architects, Matthew Brettingham and William Kent, gave it small windows to keep out the cold, and a meagre front door in the north front for the same reason, but the effect, combined with the local yellow brick with which it was built, gives Holkham Hall the chill, grim look of some closed institution. Or perhaps it was deliberate, Kent being aware of the astonishing contrast experienced when walking through that front door into what could be taken for the *Palazzo Reale* of Naples, the pink marble pillars of the entrance hall leading the visitor up the sweep of white marble steps, to the Roman statuary and the Old Master paintings displayed on the walls hung with crimson velvet and damask in the state apartments. The inlaid wood, mirrors and ormolu, the rich carpets, gold-embossed leather bindings of the books in the library, the porcelain and the silver; all is in dramatic and artful contrast to the source of such wealth: the fields beyond the windows. No wonder one Georgian visitor called it 'this *museum* of taste and elegance'.

But this grandeur did not bring happiness to its creator. Indeed, Coke, now become the first Earl of Leicester, mournfully declared, 'I am Giant of Giant's Castle'. It was his nephew, also named Thomas Coke – and Earl of Leicester (1754–1842) – who brought this great estate to its zenith. It was he who introduced new crops and farming techniques, wheat, Devon cattle and Southdown sheep to Norfolk. He made the rotation of crops compulsory in all his tenancy agreements, so that the soil would be enriched by root crops and hay returning as manure to the fields, which were given time for rest and recuperation. He reclaimed salt- marshes and held back the sea by planting the dunes so thickly and successfully that he was nicknamed 'King Pine'.

But 'Coke of Norfolk', as he became universally known, was far more than an innovative farmer on a grand scale. He was the political leader of the county, although, as a Whig, he opposed the war against the American colonies – he toasted the health of George Washington as 'The Greatest Man on Earth' – and also war with Revolutionary France, until his own country was directly threatened. He was a big, robust man in all senses, standing above the snobberies and resentments of rural society. As a contemporary song put it,

> Coke little reeks of low or high,
> Coats fine or Jackets rarely worn;
> The landlord of Holkham ne'er looks down
> On the humble growers of barley corn.

Under Coke's benevolent patronage, the growers of barley corn became less humble, for he housed his estate workers in style. The fashionable architect Samuel Wyatt was commissioned to design farm buildings, lodges and cottages that would enhance the picturesque prospect of the park. True, the agricultural authority – and future Secretary to the Board of Agriculture – Nathaniel Kent (1737 – 1810), had written to Coke in 1789: 'I own I think it as necessary to provide plain and comfortable habitations for the Poor as it is to provide comfortable and convenient buildings for cattle'. But Coke took a different view, and not only were the cottages built for his workmen comfortable and elegant, with neo-Classical trimmings, but the farmhouses he built for his tenant farmers were designed as for country gentlemen, with gravel carriage-drives sweeping to the front doors, and drawing-rooms and dining-rooms within.

Coke enjoyed the reputation of a true Norfolkman with

scant regard for the etiquette of smart society. When the Dukes of Sussex and Cambridge – the sons of King George III –stayed at Holkham, he took them shooting and it soon became apparent that one of them was a bad shot. The story was repeated around the county that, 'The keeper, who was also shooting, floored them right and left and as continually ascribed the success to the Duke, saying, "Your Royal Highness's bird". At last old Mr Coke lost all patience, and running up to the keeper, administered a kick behind, saying, "You are a lying humbug; he has not killed one and you know it".'

When Coke of Norfolk died in 1842, he was buried amongst his ancestors in the mausoleum – appropriately, it looks like a brick, lean-to farm building – alongside the little parish church at Tittleshall, where the Cokes had lived before their wealth and fame. He had brought the eighteenth century into the nineteenth and he, foremost among his fellow-landowners, their tenant farmers, architects and landscape gardeners, had changed the face of the county.

These were the three most famous landowners and estates and they set the pattern for the dozen grand families who each owned more than 10,000 acres at the end of the nineteenth century. Some occupied vast houses, rural palaces: Lord Hastings at Melton Constable, and Lord Kimberley, with a mansion of the same name. Then came more than fifty lesser landowners, also belonging to the aristocracy, such as the Earl of Albemarle at Quidenham, and the Duke of Norfolk, who lived far away in Arundel Castle, at Kenninghall. Next came the 'greater landed gentry', who owned between three and ten thousand acres; some of ancient lineage like the Fountaines, who had moved from Salle to Narford, and built a mansion there; some relatively new to Norfolk, like the future King Edward VII at Sandringham. Their names resound with Norfolk associations: Bedingfeld, Boileau, Bulwer, Ffolkes folkes, Hare, Ketton, Le Strange, Mott, Upcher, Windham and fifty more. The squirearchy, owning between two and three thousand acres, were another such roll-call: Bagge, Bentinck, Calthrop, Custance, Gurney, Cozens Hardy, Jodrell, Keppel,

Rolfe, and Unthank among them. Unlisted as landowners at the time was one of the most distinguished lines of all, the Bacons, premier baronets of England; a recent holder of the title, Sir Edmund Bacon (1903–69), Knight of the Garter and Lord Lieutenant of Norfolk, was regarded as the outstanding East Anglian of his generation, leaving the mark of his enthusiasms on agriculture and, more tangibly, on the restoration of Norwich Cathedral and the development of the University of East Anglia. Such were, and often still are, the 'county families' of Norfolk.

The boast of each established family was the great house, which with its gardens, parks, lake, follies and artfully-designed vistas, had become a peculiarly English work of art. In harmony with architecture, landscape gardening had become a profession: part agricultural, part engineering and part artistic composition. This produced great artists, notably Lancelot 'Capability' Brown (1715–83), whose work included the parks of the halls at Holkham, Melton Constable, Kimberley, Didlington and Ditchingham; and Humphry Repton (1752–1818), who worked on sixteen Norfolk estates, notably at Blickling and Holkham. His work can still be seen at Honing Hall, Wood Hall at Hilgay, on a small scale at Bracondale Lodge in Norwich, and, on a large scale, most notably, around Sheringham Hall – now owned by the National Trust – where he included hills, woods and the sea itself in a grand, sweeping composition in the Regency taste for the picturesque.

Repton was an East Anglian, born at Bury St Edmunds but living mostly in Norfolk, both in Norwich and at Sustead Old Hall. Coming to landscape design when aged nearly forty, it became a labour of love and he is said to have reduced his charges when he was particularly enjoying his work. Humphry Repton is buried in the churchyard at Aylsham beneath a little rose-garden and his epitaph – surely the most perfect for any gardener – reads,

> Not like the Egyptian tyrants – consecrate,
> Unmixt with others, shall my dust remain:
> But mould'ring, blended, melting into earth,

Mine shall give form and colour to the rose;
And while its vivid blossoms cheer mankind,
Its perfumed odour shall ascend to Heaven.

One of the most sumptuous gardens was laid out later in the century around Sandringham House, where heathland on the estate was planted with heather in the vain hope of breeding grouse for the shooting parties, which, then and now, slaughter colossal numbers of half-tame game-birds. Sandringham had been bought by Queen Victoria in 1861 and the house rebuilt in Jacobean style for the Prince of Wales, who, as King Edward VII, was the first monarch to regard it as a private home; and, later, three successive monarchs liked to spend Christmas there. It remains a private house rather than a palace but the grounds are open to the public.

However splendid the parks and gardens, it was the great houses and their inhabitants that gave the county much of its character. Indeed, they seemed to assume a life and character of their own, absorbed from generations of occupants and their tastes and achievements, and those of their guests, whether other inhabitants of other such houses, the London literati or those assembled for balls and shooting parties. A family might fade, or run to seed, but the great house, embowered in its park and farmland would, at least for a time, live on, radiating the sense of stability and economic and social power that first raised it up. Even when the great house itself was gone, as at Didlington near Swaffham, something of the corporate soul of those who created, tended and inhabited it seems to survive in the woods, lakes and follies.

The country house was – but now seldom is – a society in microcosm. Aside from its satellite farms, the house, garden, kitchen garden and park, it had its own indigenous population. It has survived in a muted manner but its heyday was in the reigns of Queen Victoria and her son. There was, at its centre, The Family, who owned it and were attended upon by their staff, indoors and out of doors, who might number anything from twenty to fifty; far more with their dependents. Service in such an establishment was prized as giving security, food and shelter. However hard the maids might be worked by the housekeeper, they at least had meals and warmth in the servants' hall and their own little bedroom in the attic. Beyond the green baize door that would separate The Family from their staff was a parallel social order, presided over by the butler and the cook and its members were, usually, contented enough, each knowing his or her place in the social order of house, county and country.

These were two separate but interlocking worlds. The children of the staff would remember it as fondly as those of The Family but from a different perspective. One of the former has written to me of her early memories. 'For all the children of the hamlet, Didlington Hall and Park was a kind of "Mecca", the golden sandy drive winding to the red brick mansion in its beautiful green setting. The avenue of magnificent limes, the mysterious "ice-house", the little copse to the left of the drive in spring literally carpeted with primroses and in autumn the beeches, their glory reflected in the lake, which when frozen in winter enabled us to slide across to the Folly in the middle . . . There was otter-hunting in the Wissey, which we were allowed to watch, sitting on the bridges in utter silence. Beyond the trout stream the Wood Close for chestnuts and blackberries. The wood between the bridges provided an endless supply of firewood . . . As children we never saw inside the Hall.'

There were also the governesses and, less frequently, the tutors. These were intelligent but impecunious young people from the middle class, sometimes the children of clergymen, who educated the children in the schoolroom of the big house, from which the boys would be sent to their public schools. Occasionally, these worlds would overlap and lowered voices would report that 'he married his cook', or 'she was a governess, you know'. When a pretty housemaid confided to the cook that she was pregnant, it was sometimes the young men of the ruling family who were suspected and who occasionally admitted as much. When Lady Margaret Douglas-Home, the daughter of the Earl Spencer, who owned land in north-west Norfolk, recalled her childhood, she wrote that, 'My Nannie's father and my Nannie herself showed a striking resemblance to many of the red-haired Spencers. In our walks and drives outside the Park, I was constantly taken for her daughter, we looked so alike. It never occurred to me then, it only has now!'

One Norfolk friend of mine had a broad Norfolk accent, skilled manual employment and remarkably distinguished looks, which might have marked him down as a fine-looking officer in a fashionable regiment; his mother had been in service at the big house and the family there had kept an attentive eye on his upbringing; occasionally, a famous county name was whispered in the village but never in his hearing. Such cross-fertilisation gave variety to the genes of both great family and village.

It was when the nation finally called to the grooms and bootboys and gardeners – and to the sons of The Families – to fight in the two world wars that this social structure cracked and crumbled, while its component parts held firm. While it had lasted, it had been reassuring to all concerned. Before breakfast, the staff, led by the butler and cook, would file in to the dining-room to join The Family and their guests at morning prayer, kneeling upon the seats of chairs ranged round the room and facing the wall. Whereupon the head of the household would read brief prayers, so setting the day in the context of eternal verities before the staff filed out to their duties, but not before setting the chairs around the table so that breakfast could begin. This little ceremony, which had seemed to set the seal on a divinely ordained social order, survived here and there until the Second World War.

There was always a drawing together of the inhabitants of the big houses, as if they dreaded the uncertainties of the world beyond the park wall. Old nannies would be kept as pensioners in such houses for the remainder of their lives, still loved by those they had once ruled in the nursery. The children of servants would often themselves be taken into service, although perhaps at a neighbouring house. Some time in the 1950s, I met an old man, who, I remembered, had once combined the jobs of gamekeeper and chauffeur at a country house where my parents and I had sometimes been guests two decades earlier, and, in the changed world of the time, he remarked, 'There's not so many like us left, is there, sir?' It was a recognition of a mutual understanding within the constraints of the structure in which we had once found ourselves.

The keepers, footmen, grooms, bootboys and the rest had marched off to the Great War, and those who returned were often inspired by higher aspirations. They were sometimes of better human stock than their employers and, if the spur of ambition was in them, their knowledge of the ways of those known as 'their betters' could sometimes help them to success. Many were the sons of those 'in service' who entered the professions; the opportunities for daughters were still, of course, restricted.

Not all employers set good examples. There were rakes and ne'er-do-wells in the aristocracy and the landed gentry, from the duellists and libertines of the seventeenth and eighteenth centuries to the gamblers and spendthrifts of more recent times. A splendid inheritance, or dynasty, could be damaged by eccentricity. There was for example, in the last century, poor 'Mad' William Windham of Felbrigg, who squandered his inheritance, and whose greatest pleasure was to drive the stage-coach at full tilt through Norfolk villages between Cromer and Norwich for wages of a guinea a week. Then, at Colney Hall in 1911 one of the Barclays was killed by his sister's pet lion, when he returned after a long absence.

Not all landowners came from ancient lines rooted in the soil. Sometimes the owners of great houses had made their approach to grandeur through what was disparagingly known as 'trade' and this had to be 'lived down'. Yet many such enabled the houses and estates to survive. Throughout the twentieth century about a hundred and ten estates were sold or broken up but a dozen more than that number survived. In that time more than fifty great houses were demolished but, at the end of the century, between four and five hundred large old houses survive in the county. Six of the grandest are open to the public on a regular basis – including Holkham and three great houses owned by the National Trust: Blickling, Felbrigg and Oxborough; others open their grounds for the study of the historical development of parks and gardens, or just for walking through beautiful country.

Owning, or tilling the land, was not, of course, the only way the people of Norfolk supported themselves, although it had always been the most socially desirable as well as the most reliable source of economic and political power. Hunting and fishing had priority and, after the first crops were grown, came the development of industry. It was an ancient history.

The first industrial site in the county – and one of the first in England – is still extraordinary. From the air, it looks like the scene of a twentieth-century battle: a great expanse of craters blown by bombs and overgrown by grass. The craters are, in fact, collapsed mine shafts sunk by Stone Age men in search of flints from which to fashion tools and weapons. The mines have, for centuries now, been known as Grimes Graves and they lie to the north of Brandon on the Suffolk border. Such can be the telescoping of history hereabouts that, when I first came upon such a crater at a favourite picnic halt on the edge of Emily's Wood nearby, I thought it dated from the Second World War and had been caused by a bomber crashing with a full load of bombs.

The flint mines were worked more than two millennia before Christ. Flints had presumably first been picked up on the surface and then, perhaps, a land-slip showed a stratum, sometimes 30 feet deep. Shafts were sunk to this level, a working chamber excavated and, from this, galleries driven laterally through the soft, sandy soil. The flintstones were brought to the surface to be chipped into the required shapes.

Through the centuries East Anglia conducted the industries introduced by its conquerors from the Continent, as is shown by the Roman pottery and Saxon metalwork that are un-earthed. Then, as sheep and their wool became a principal product of the farms, textiles followed. Norwich became a manufacturing town thanks to this industry and the village of Worstead gave its name to a cloth that has survived the centuries. Mostly, the yarn was spun from the raw wool in the villages, and woven and finished in Norwich, where the number of skilled weavers was increased during the sixteenth century by the influx of some 6,000 Dutch refugees – 'the strangers', as they were known – fleeing Spanish religious persecution in the Netherlands. By the beginning of the seventeenth century the population had grown to about 32,000, half of which was engaged in the textiles industry. So busy was the city that Daniel Defoe, visiting Norwich in 1722, could write, 'If a stranger were to ride through, or view, the city of Norwich, he would have reason to think that here was a town without inhabitants . . . the inhabitants being all busy at their manufacture, dwell in their combing-shops, twisting mills and other work houses'.

Norfolk had no coal, of course, so the main tide of the Industrial Revolution passed it by. As competition from the north of England increased with mechanisation, the Norwich textile workshops concentrated on quality, weaving cloth of worsted mixed with silk or cotton, embroidery and dyeing, and also producing light, newly-fashioned shawls. Light and attractive as it was, Norwich cloth could not indefinitely compete with the Lancashire mills and was eventually superseded.

However, Norwich could, by the eighteenth century, support other industries to meet its own needs and for export. Two of the other principal industries were tanning and leatherwork, leading to shoemaking, and malting and brewing (every village had its pub, the bigger villages several, while Norwich had more than 600 by the end of the nineteenth century). The city was rich enough to breed a trade in luxuries and, in the late sixteenth and throughout the seventeenth centuries, silversmiths were flourishing there. Yet it also remained a rural market-town and weekly sales of livestock were held in the great cattle market on the far side of the castle from its daily produce market.

Both agriculture and manufacturing industry depended, of course, upon transport. Until the middle of the nineteenth century this had been by water whenever possible, the sea ports shipping produce and products, sailing wherries and barges carrying loads inland on rivers and canals. Roads were poor, but wagons hauled goods along them, and livestock had to walk to market and slaughter, even as far as London: vast flocks of ducks and geese were made to waddle through warm tar and then sand to harden their feet before journeys of over a hundred miles.

Then came the railways, beginning in 1844 with a line linking Norwich with Great Yarmouth; followed a year later with another from Norwich to Brandon and thence to London. A decade later, the major centres were linked and even the remote north coast was reached by a line from Fakenham to Wells. In 1862 the county's railway companies were merged into the Great Eastern Railway; finally, in 1906, the network was complete, with Blakeney the only small town without a railway station within five miles. There was a central railway junction and marshalling yards and workshops at Melton Constable, where terraces of cottages were built for railway workers, giving it the look of the Midlands industrial towns.

With the county almost completely covered by the railways, farmers and manufacturers could send their goods to market with far greater ease. This aroused the frustrated anger of the wherrymen of East Norfolk, as Rider Haggard discovered when he stood for Parliament in 1895 and rashly advocated subsidies to help farmers send their produce to market by rail. However, the railways remained a major cohesive force, both economic and social. Almost anywhere in Norfolk could be reached by a three-and-a-half-hour journey from London, changing from a comfortable express with a dining-car at one of the stations between Liverpool Street and Norwich, or King's Lynn, to a little puffing train on a branch line. Norfolk people went visiting friends in the county by the meandering rails, when a journey by motor car would take hours, particularly with the prevailing risks of punctures on the poor roads, or a 'breakdown'. One such branch line, running from Heacham to Wells via the villages of 'High Norfolk', exported the district's cattle and sheep, grain, vegetables, shellfish and Holkham bricks; importing coal, oil and cattle feed. The railway lines seemed to hold Norfolk together, like the roots of a tree binding a river bank.

Then, in 1963, the Government accepted the report on the rationalisation of the railways by Dr Beeching and over the next five years most of the Norfolk system was abandoned and uprooted. What remained of the noble concept was a skeleton, linking London and the Midlands with Norwich and King's Lynn and the stations along those lines, and maintaining a fragile link with Great Yarmouth and Cromer. Passengers and commercial traffic were forced on to the roads and the M11 motorway from London swept close to the county border. Within Norfolk, contrary to promises, the branch lines were not replaced by adequate bus services, so that here, as throughout the United Kingdom, the car and lorry are dominant.

The possibility of air travel was slow to dawn long after the advent of flight itself. In March 1783 several balloon ascents were made from Norwich, causing much surprise but no prophecies of what might eventually follow; certainly not by Silas Neville, a doctor in the city. 'Saw a large Air Balloon launched from Burn's garden near the river; it was lost in the clouds in a shower of hail in two minutes 30 seconds,' he wrote in his diary, and, a fortnight later, 'At Quantrill's garden, another balloon launched. The mania for these things is very general at present, but *cui bono*? To what use can they be applied?' Even in 1922, long after heavier-than-air aviation was well-established, Sir Rider Haggard declared, 'Nothing will make me believe that these air craft are desirable vehicles of locomotion'.

Other means of communication developed and, by the middle of the century, the telegraph supplemented the postal service. 'While riding through Longham, I perceived the posts and wires of an electric telegraph stretching across the fields from the chief farmer's house to the parsonage,' noted a Norfolk clergyman in 1852.

Fearing that a railway was in contemplation, I enquired of a labouring man a solution of the enigma. 'Sir', he replied (with a most knowing look, and indicating the houses with his forefinger), 'there be a young gentleman as lives here, and a young lady as lives there, and they tell me' (looking incredulous) 'that they talk to one another by means of them wires.' What would our forefathers have thought of making love by means of an electric telegraph!

The spread of communications – notably the railways – over a century had, of course, encouraged the development of engineering from its simple origins. It grew from the number of blacksmiths and metalworkers required to service the horse, coach and wagon traffic the city generated and to provide the increasingly complex machinery required on the farms. Out of this eventually grew sophisticated engineering manufacturers, like Boulton and Paul, which built fighter aircraft for both world wars. Yet the traces of the old weavers survived, and, during the Second World War, Norwich was producing silk for parachutes. Engineering kept a toe-hold in Norfolk but it was always to be on a generally modest scale. Fifty years on, elderly people in Burnham Market still talk with pride of their 'war factory', although it was little more than a shed and manufactured hinges for spectacles.

The ancient capital, Thetford, was farther from the sea than Norwich, although goods could be shipped there slowly by river and then canal. So farm products – notably grain for malt and then brewing – remained its staple until paper-milling began in the eighteenth century and it was then that engineering was introduced. But it was not founded on any natural advantage such as coal, or proximity to water transport but on the need for agricultural machinery. It grew in a single firm, Burrell's, which became the leading manufacturers of traction engines not only in Britain but in the world. But the fortunes of Burrell's declined with those of the steam engine and, in 1928, the Thetford factory closed. Engineering was started in other Norfolk towns: agricultural machinery made in Dereham, steam engines in Lynn and printing works were set up in Fakenham, for example. Some fifty small towns and villages had their own iron foundries.

The revival of Thetford kept pace with the growth of the conifer forests planted by the Forestry Commission on the surrounding Breckland heaths. After the Second World War, furniture-making was amongst new industries established there to employ an influx of workers from an over-populated

London. Other industries were introduced there and to other Norfolk towns, often to help employ more 'overspill' populations to an extent that London accents became almost as common as Norfolk accents among the crowds in the supermarkets, and in Thetford more so. Indeed, that expansion swamped the old town with what its indigenous inhabitants regarded as foreigners, its population being more than quadrupled. This influx was combined with the establishing of light manufacturing industries, their products including electrical and plastic goods, as well as furniture. In the boom years of the 1980s Thetford flourished only to be hit by the recession and consequent unemployment, for which city-bred workers were particularly ill-suited. In King's Lynn, industries linked with agriculture included a soup factory and canning works and each of the larger market towns grew its own industrial estate; all suffered in the recession at the beginning of the 1990s.

Great Yarmouth was fortunate in taking its share of the newly-discovered riches of the North Sea when selected as the base for the extraction of natural gas with the pipeline terminal on the coast at Bacton; this industry survived as others fell to the recession. Factories closed in Norwich, too, but it was fortunate in having the Norwich Union insurance company; other 'white collar' employers, including the Stationery Office and the Central Computer Agency of the Civil Service, became its major employers, rather than manufacturing industry.

Meanwhile tourism became the growth industry, employing more than any other in North Norfolk by 1990. Caravan parks proliferated on the coast; pleasure-boats on the Broads; small hotels and guest-houses and pubs flourished, as did all the service industries catering for visitors. In a way, this was fitting because, early in the century, a final drawing-together of farming, business and the influx of outsiders had been symbolised by the building of the last great country mansion in Norfolk: Sennowe Park.

Built with the fortune made from international tourism by Thomas Cook, it arose as a rival to Houghton and Holkham. The grandson of the founder of the travel company, and the son of the Thomas Cook who used that company to transport the relief expedition up the Nile in the hope of saving General Gordon in Khartoum, decided to sell his interest in the business and set himself up as a Norfolk landowner with mansion to match. This Thomas Cook was eccentric but not always lovable, and on his visits to Fakenham he enjoyed heating a shovel-full of copper pennies over the fire in The Crown inn, then tossing them across the market square to watch little boys burn their fingers as they scrambled for the coins.

The house he planned was suitably eccentric. It was to be built around an eighteenth-century house – itself enough for any Norfolk landowner, for it had once belonged to the Kimberleys, but not for an Edwardian grandee – standing on a spur above a hidden, wooded valley and would command a view of a new eight-acre lake. Designed by George Skipper, the Norfolk architect who Sir John Betjeman said was 'to Norwich what Gaudi was to Barcelona', it was to be a *palazzo*. Indeed, he imported a team of Italian masons and carvers to create the elaborate terraces on which the house would stand, as well as the statuary, columns, urns, balustrades and stone garlands that would adorn it. An ostentatious, florid fantasy, incorporating various styles – Tudor, English Renaissance, Georgian, neo-Classical and Art Nouveau – it was vast and designed for entertaining, which, after its completion in 1908, duly began. There was always a touch of vulgarity about it: when Cook installed a searchlight on top of the enormous water-tower to enable him and his guests to shoot duck on the lake by night, the coastguard ordered it to be removed, as ships' captains out in the North Sea, fifteen miles away, had mistaken it for a lighthouse.

But, just as the builder of Sennowe had hoped, the Cooks did become landed gentry as the mansion, the park and the twenty-three farms on the estate were handed down the generations. The present owner, Mr Tom Cook, lives in the great house but is himself a practical and successful farmer, a member of the Rural Development Commission, and he has been High Sheriff of the county. There should be nothing surprising about this. The Cooks have only repeated a pattern set by the Saxons, the Danes and the Normans.

The second half of the twentieth century, since the two global wars, brought about many changes in Norfolk. Some of the great estates were broken up and mansions demolished – fifty-four of them since the end of the Second World War – or allowed to fall into ruin, or disrepair, while a few, like Gunton, managed to survive by conversion for multi-occupation. Sometimes this was brought about by the dying out of a landed family. One of the greatest houses, Melton Constable, was lost to the Astley family after nearly three centuries when sold in 1965 by the head of the family, Lord Hastings. But he was no run-to-seed relic of the former ruling class; described as a 'masterful' landowner, he had commanded a battalion of the Home Guard during the Second World War, been chairman of the Norfolk Agricultural Research Station for forty-four years and his reaction to bureaucracy had been, 'The man who invented ink, gentlemen, should have been drowned in it – drowned in it!'

Yet new demands and new technology did produce new branches of agriculture and its dependant industry. One was the demand for sugar beet for refining and another for fruit and vegetables to be canned or frozen. The development of 'factory farming' meant changing the face of the countryside as livestock that had once roamed the fields and farmyards were confined to long huts reminiscent of those in concentration camps. This did not necessarily involve cruelty but it did involve industrialisation.

One example of this was that transformation of what had been, relatively, the luxury trade of turkey-farming into mass-production for mass markets by the initiative of a single Norfolkman, Bernard Matthews (b. 1930). Born into a poor country family near Norwich, young Bernard showed such promise that neighbours helped support him through his schooldays and he rewarded their faith by his industry. At the age of eighteen, he spent £2 10s on a few turkey eggs and a simple incubator and within forty years had built up a turkey-farming company valued at £150,000,000. By the mid-1990s, he always had more than 10,000,000 turkeys filling four hundred turkey-houses, mostly in Norfolk, and had expanded his turkey-empire with another million in Hungary. This one farmer had changed the turkey from the Christmas treat to the daily diet for mass-consumption.

The mechanisation of the farms has meant that, in that time, the total of more than 40,000 farm workers has been cut by a quarter. As cottages became vacant they were bought as second homes for the urban middle class in such numbers that coastal villages lost their strong characters. Some small market towns – notably Holt and Burnham Market – seemed to be given over to the welfare of the affluent 'incomers', their former smithies and forges, their saddlers', chandlers', iron-mongers' and drapers' shops being converted into fashion boutiques, 'gift' shops, delicatessens, antique shops and estate agents' offices. Such towns became suburbanised with car parks, or lines painted on their roads to denote areas for parking, concrete kerbs set around greens and public lavatories built; bungalows proliferated in the outskirts; elaborate carved wooden village signs, inspired by local legend, were commissioned. Alehouses were converted into smart restaurants, a noteworthy example being the tiny Ordnance Arms, near Guist, which became a successful Thai restaurant.

Meanwhile, the population, which had been sparse since the Middle Ages, began to increase rapidly – at four times the national average towards the end of the century – almost all of this being imported. King's Lynn and Thetford had agreed to take the 'overspill' of London's population and the attendant social problems; Fakenham, Diss and North Walsham became 'growth centres' with plans for new light industry; while several smaller market towns were, according to viewpoint, promised, or threatened with, expansion. Excessive housing development was allowed throughout the county, one-third of the new settlers being of retirement age; the rest – often affluent after buying a house in Norfolk for less than half the price for which they sold their former home elsewhere – being able to compete for the available employment. Norwich became a metropolis for, while the old city within the line of the medieval walls remained much as it was after the destruction of the Second World War and consequent post-war development, the suburbs spread across fields and woodland, swallowing up villages. Its population of about 114,000 at the beginning of the century had only increased by some 15,000 by the end, but the city's suburban sprawl had spread to cover something like eight miles by six.

One consequence of a shifting and expanding population was, here as elsewhere, an epidemic of crime. With the county constabulary one of the most under-funded in the country, policing standards fell towards the end of the twentieth century. The resident constable disappeared from villages and was replaced by the lone policeman in a patrol car, while many of the remaining police stations were manned only during office hours. Not only remote country houses and empty holiday cottages were plundered by burglars but 'smash-and-grab' attacks and 'ram-raiding' became a threat to shops in market towns. Owners of both town and country houses have often come to the conclusion that the latter are at greater risk.

Even the landscape, which had seemed timeless and had altered little since it had been recorded in water-colour by the artists of the Norwich School, changed. Indeed, it was said that across much of the country three-quarters of the land-scape features marked on Victorian maps had disappeared. Half the county's hedgerows had been uprooted to convert the familiar pattern of small fields, copses, ponds and woodland into prairies convenient to mechanised farming. From these the topsoil would be carried away in clouds of dust when the wind blew in times of drought. This land was drenched with herbicides, pesticides and fertilising chemicals, notably nitrates, which leached into the subterranean aquifers, pollut-ing the supply of drinking water. Some farmers, reluctant to grow crops suited to a dry climate, drew vast quantities of water from bore-holes, reducing the flow of smaller rivers, already lowered by drought, so that some dried up completely. There was talk of the 'greenhouse effect' of man-made gases changing the climate, producing chronic drought but also raising the level of the sea to inundate the low-lying east coast. Then, in the early 1990s, persistent rain began again, the aquifers refilled, the rivers flowed and there was less speculation about climatic change. There was, however, another change: the countryside was quiet and sometimes silent, for few birds sang. The uprooting of the hedgerows had removed their habitat and the use of herbicides and pesticides had destroyed their food; the numbers of many species fell by half. As the end of the twentieth century approaches, the song of the lark is rare.

III
Sea

When Captain Horatio Nelson was exiled, unemployed and on half-pay, in his native village of Burnham Thorpe for five years before the outbreak of war with Revolutionary France in 1793, he had a favourite walk. From the Parsonage, he would take the lane that ran past the stables and across fields to the crest of a low chalk ridge behind it. From there he could look north and, between the gentle, sloping shoulders of the downs, he could see the sea.

It was just a short line of horizon, sometimes blue, sometimes grey, but it was a link with the world beyond and the destiny he was convinced was his. Often, that stretch of sea was flecked with sails, occasionally crowded as when the long-awaited change of wind released a fleet of colliers from the Tyne, or the herring fleet sailed north from Great Yarmouth, or a brisk south-westerly bore a flock of merchantmen to or from the Thames and the Baltic.

The sea was the source of both wealth and danger. For Norfolk people, it bore trade with other parts of the British Isles and with the Continent. It was also the carrier of invaders – German tribes, Danes and then, centuries later, French and Germans – and, gentle as that shore could seem, there was the danger of the sea itself. The shallows off the Norfolk coast might shelter ships at anchor in familiar roadsteads but they could also tear ships apart.

Typical of the treachery of this coast was the fate of one of Nelson's own ships, the *Invincible*, a ship of the line mounting seventy-four guns, which was on passage to join him off Copenhagen in the spring of 1801. Sailing in fine, clear weather just out of sight of the tall tower of Happisburgh church – a familiar landmark to generations of sailors – her course had been set through the channels dividing a group of sandbanks. She was off-course, ran aground and, heavily laden with ordnance for the Baltic, was held fast. Her boats were hoisted out in case she had to be abandoned but her captain was confident that she could be floated on the next tide. Then a gale blew up, swept away her boats and all hope of escape, and began to break up the ship. Next day she slid off the shoal and sank in deep water with the loss of more than four hundred lives.

Stories like that – albeit seldom so disastrous – are familiar on this coast. More familiar are accounts of activities suggested by the words of a toast painted across china punch-bowls: 'Success to Trade'. Far back, before Nelson's life-time, a little harbour had evolved on the coast wherever a river ran into the sea. These had been probed by the Danish longships as access to virgin plundering-grounds. They sailed past Burnham Overy towards Burnham Thorpe, where uneven turf is all that remains of a prosperous settlement: was it the Danes, or was it a later plague, that made the surviving villagers rebuild it on the far side of the church? The invaders landed somewhere nearby and fought a fierce battle with the defending Saxons on high ground above South Creake that is still called Bloodgate. Certainly, there was a vast, round fort of earthworks and ditches there, flattened by farming in the last century – unlike the similar fort at Warham, which is only a third of its size – and can now only be seen from the air when the state of the crops betray the distant past.

They sailed up another creek through the salt-marshes and built a fort beside it at a bleak place they named Holkham, which meant 'Ship Town'. At Burnham Overy Staithe, they used to tell a ghost story of the square sail of a Viking ship being seen above the line of the sand dunes and of a helmeted Viking met on the beach. Even with an awareness of what must have been vulnerable estuaries, high ground named Beacon Hill, uneven fields where villages once stood, and the earthworks, it is difficult to imagine the recurrent holocausts that followed the sighting of those square sails on the eastern horizon.

When peace was finally restored after the Norman conquest, ports mostly developed at the mouths of estuaries, not only at King's Lynn and Great Yarmouth but, between them, at Burnham Overy, Wells, Blakeney and Cley, and goods were even manhandled across the beaches at Dersingham and Snettisham on the Wash, and at Cromer. Some of the small ports had assumed considerable importance by the sixteenth century and Burnham Overy was once said to be the best harbour between Harwich and Newcastle. At that time, British shipping began to take trade from the Dutch and the number of seafarers grew accordingly: in 1582 it was recorded that 232 shipmasters lived in Norfolk (as against 93 in Suffolk and 143 in London) and that 1,570 of the 15,454 seamen registered in England lived in Norfolk, while there were only 1,196 in Suffolk and 2,281 in London, half of them Thames watermen. All were kept busy exporting, in particular, corn, barley, cloth and herrings, and importing coal, stone and Dutch pottery.

The two principal ports, King's Lynn and Great Yarmouth, began in the same way as the other settlements, at the mouths of rivers; in their cases, the Ouse and the Wensum respectively. The former bore the riverine trade of Ely, Peterborough and Cambridge and, after the draining of the Fens in the seventeenth century, the harvests of that rich, dark earth. The latter was the port for Norwich, inland and upstream, with the greatest markets in all Norfolk, and its manufactories initially exported cloth woven from Norfolk wool.

Lynn – known as Bishop's Lynn (meaning bishop's lake) before the dissolution of the monasteries by King Henry VIII – assumed over the centuries touches of Venice, Amsterdam and the Hanseatic ports across the North Sea. Depending upon waterborne trade, its merchants built themselves grand houses backing on to, rather than above, their warehouses and also displayed their wealth and worthiness in magnificent churches. Lynn exported its own salt and goods brought down the river Ouse from the towns, farms and mines to the west: grain from the fenland, wool and cloth from inland Norfolk and the Midlands and lead from Derbyshire mines. In turn it was the entrepot for Scandinavian timber, hemp and coal, French wine, Flemish cloth and Russian furs and more delicate luxuries like Dutch pottery and Venetian glass. Even in the twentieth century, grain and timber were handled in quantity by the little port but the main industry of the town had become the canning and freezing of vegetables and fruit from market-gardens and orchards inland.

Down the centuries, prosperity generated a cultural tradition and, since the Second World War, the annual King's Lynn Festival has become one of the most celebrated musical, theatrical and artistic jamborees in the country. Sadly, during that same period, the old centre of the town has been demolished and replaced by a huge, vulgar, redbrick 'shopping precinct' that might belong to any industrial town anywhere, mercifully sparing the glorious old streets and squares along the muddy bank of the Great Ouse.

Yarmouth, also rich, was kept closer to the smell of tar, hemp and fishing nets by its great herring fleet, by its position on a spit between its harbour in the river to one side and the open sea to the other, and by its exposure to the threat of attack from across the North Sea.

Although Great Yarmouth was, and is, the principal port of Norfolk, its fortunes were founded as much on this fishery as on its trade. Already in the thirteenth century, herrings were being salted and smoked there for packing and export, and three heraldic herrings decorated the town's coat of arms. The Yarmouth fishing fleet was numbered in hundreds, its fortunes founded on two seasons: herrings in autumn and mackerel in spring. First, smacks with tan sails, then, steam drifters, were based there – more than 1,600 when Scottish boats were working out of the port just before the first World War; 900,000,000 herring were landed in 1913 – while several thousand fisher girls waited ashore to gut and pack their catch. Its great days were in the nineteenth and early twentieth centuries for then the two world wars, in which the North Sea was the arena for naval contest between Britain and Germany, disrupted fishing. In the subsequent peace, the shallow sea was over-fished.

The fishery ensured that Yarmouth could not succeed as a fashionable seaside holiday resort. An attempt to make it so in the eighteenth century failed. 'To Yarmouth', noted Silas Neville, an enthusiastic tourist, in 1783, 'which has for some years been a great bathing place and is amazingly brushed up. It is very cold and smells delightfully of herrings.' It did not attract a profitable tourist trade until the railway brought the less affluent families from Norwich and beyond in the middle of the next century and the town had grown large enough to site its seaside entertainments beyond the wafting smells from the fish-quays.

Both towns thrived on the export of Norfolk wool to the Netherlands for weaving and importing the resulting cloth, together with Dutch pottery and even bulbs when the seventeenth century 'tulipomania' infected the Dutch engineers working on land-reclamation in East Anglia. Both unloaded Baltic timber, hemp, pitch, tar and iron and furs, but Lynn had its own industry in the production of salt from the shallows of the Wash for preserving meat and fish.

Not all trading partners were across the North Sea, for most transport of merchandise within the British Isles was seaborne, particularly coal from the Tyne. If a Norfolk gentleman needed to buy furniture from London, he would probably have it sent by sea; such trade, in particular, passed through the little ports to be moved inland by wagon.

Neither port was easy of access. Lynn could, and can, only be reached by navigating channels between the sandbanks of the Wash and the approaches to Yarmouth are barred by shoals, the nearest of which, Scroby Sands, served a useful purpose by sheltering the deep water off the town which became Yarmouth Roads. But whereas Lynn also served as a market town for west Norfolk and its estates, the hinterland of Yarmouth was the flatlands and lagoons known as the Broads, while the markets in Norwich, seventeen miles inland, overshadowed all others in the east of the county; it was therefore first and last a seaport.

Yarmouth grew on its three-mile spit of sand between the river Yare – its flow strengthened by the Wensum from

Norwich – and the sea. At right-angles to the beach and the streets, little houses lined alleys called The Rows and, along the bank of the river, where shipping discharged their cargoes, the merchants' houses were built. Nowadays, amongst the chain stores and the smell of hamburgers and candyfloss, it is difficult to imagine the Yarmouth that our great-grandparents knew.

Further back, the flavour of Yarmouth early in the last century can be found most pungently in the pages of *David Copperfield*, for it was there that Charles Dickens introduced the boy to the Peggotty family. 'I was quite tired and very glad when we saw Yarmouth,' remembered David.

> It looked rather spongy and soppy, I thought, as I carried my eye over the great, dull waste that lay across the river . . . As we drew a little nearer and saw the whole adjacent prospect lying a straight low line under the sky, I hinted to Peggotty . . . that if the land had been a little more separated from the sea, and the town and the tide had not been quite so much mixed up, like toast and water, it would have been nicer.

But when they entered the town and 'smelt the fish, and pitch, and oakum, and tar and saw the sailors walking about, and the carts jingling up and down over the stones, I felt . . . that Yarmouth was, upon the whole, the finest place in the universe'.

Then David was introduced to Peggotty's home in an upturned boat and was enchanted by the cosiness of its interior and, in particular, by the pictures on the wooden walls:

> Abraham in red going to sacrifice Isaac in blue, and Daniel in yellow cast into a den of green lions . . . a picture of the *Sarah Jane* lugger, built at Sunderland, with a real, little wooden stern stuck on to it; a work of art, combining composition with carpentry, which I considered to be one of the most enviable possessions the world could afford.

But the little boat-house had one snag: 'the smell of fish; which was so searching that when I took out my pocket-handkerchief to wipe my nose, I found it smelt exactly as if it had wrapped up a lobster'. Nowadays a predominant smell in Yarmouth is the waft of warm, fish-scented frying-fat.

A particularly pungent myth of the seaside is that of

smugglers and smuggling. It was never quite such a legend in
Norfolk as in Kent or Sussex, which were a short run from the
French coast, but since transport by sea cost only time and
wages in the days of sail, the lonely beaches of East Anglia
were worth a detour. Tax-avoidance has always been popular
and was not confined to the criminal classes. In Norfolk,
Parson Woodforde of Weston Longville relied upon
smugglers for his little luxuries, a typical entry in his diary
reading, 'Andrews the Smuggler brought me this night about
11 o'clock a bagg of Hyson Tea 6 Pd. weight. He frightened us
a little by whistling under the Parlour windows just as we were
going to bed. I gave him some Geneva and paid him for the tea
at 10/6 per Pd.'

The trade was winked at by rural worthies. One nineteenth-
century vicar of Gorleston wrote,

> Beneath my feet as I write are large and airy cellars, once used for the
> storage of imported goods and, until a few years ago, a subterranean
> passage connected these with a landing-stage by the waterside: let the full
> truth be told, the designer of all was the vicar of the parish and this house
> was, and still is, the vicarage.

Yet the parsons and squires who patronised the smugglers
were probably unaware of the means by which their tea,
brandy, wine, tobacco, spice and linen reached them. Brought
across the North Sea from the Low Countries or France in
small sailing ships, the problem arose in getting the contraband ashore for there were no isolated, rocky coves as in the
West Country. So one favoured method was to load it into a
boat and anchor just above the low water mark, so that, when
the tide was fully ebbed, she lay on the sand. Then a familiar
horse and cart, used to gather seaweed for spreading on fields
as fertiliser, would be led across the sands at dawn to load the
contraband and seaweed pitchforked on top of it. Once on dry
land, there would be plenty of secluded lanes leading to lonely
barns, or even church crypts, where it could be stored.
Distribution across the county and country was well
organised, one of the principal centres of the trade being North
Walsham, which was linked by a network of tracks suitable
for pack-horses leading to London, Peterborough and the

Midlands. On the far side of the county, a green lane runs between hedges past Wood Farm, the site of the novelist Rider Haggard's birthplace at West Bradenham near Swaffham and there is no reason to doubt that it was called Smuggler's Lane because it was once the route for contraband bound from the coast to Cambridge.

It was a colossal business and the Government estimated that duty was paid on less than a quarter of imported luxuries. The only means of controlling smuggling was the military arm of the Excise Service. Revenue cutters at sea, coastguards and riding officers, sometimes supported by dragoons, ashore did their best to interdict the trade. Far from being a romantic business of 'Turn to the wall, my darling, as the gentlemen ride by', it was often an ugly business of savage skirmishes in the dark. A dragoon was buried in Hunstanton churchyard in 1784, his headstone telling how he was 'shot from his horse by a party of Smugglers':

> Four balls thro' me Pearced there way:
> Hard it was. I'd no time to pray.

It was not until what was then called the Great War with France had been won that the resources were available to recruit and house a strong coastguard and establish some control. Stoutly-built rows of coastguard cottages and head-stones in seaside churchyards commemorate a conflict of interests involving whole communities.

The seaside was not seen as a place for recreation until the eighteenth century when 'watering places' became the fashion, and among the first of these was Cromer, where fishermen launched their boats from the shingle beach. It was a simple, busy place as one traveller wrote, 'there is no harbour at Cromer, yet corn is exported and coals, deals, etc., received in return. The vessels used are 60 to 100 tons burden . . . at high water they are laid upon the beach and, as soon as the water is sufficiently ebbed, carts are drawn to the side of the ship and the coals shot into them.' This visitor did not think it had much to offer: 'The Norfolk Tourist has done what he can for Cromer, desiring their readers will suffer its situation and the

Imprints of unrecorded history: the Iron Age fort built by the Iceni at Warham near the north coast of Norfolk. (*Photo: Aerial Photography Publications*)

Monuments to recorded history: Norman order centred on buildings like the castle and cathedral at Norwich. (*Photo: Aerial Photography Publications*)

The threatening sea: rescue off Gorleston by Captain Manby's breeches buoy, painted by John Cantilloe Joy (c1806–60). (*Norfolk Museums Service*)

The vulnerable shore: beaches, such as at Cley, were ideal for beaching the Vikings' longships. (*Photo: Dona Haycraft*)

Wealth and power were displayed by using land for parks and avenues as at Langley Park, painted in 1749 by John Wootton (1682–1764). (*Norfolk Museums Service*)

The great avenue at Holkham stretches for two miles from a triumphal arch to Coke of Norfolk's mansion. (*Photo: Dona Haycraft*)

The Scole Inn – seen in this engraving of 1740 after a painting by Joshua Kirby – was a prototype hotel and its sign foreshadowed roadside advertising. (*Norfolk Museums Service*)

Fear of revolution: local radicals make 'John Bull' kneel before French revolutionaries in a caricature by James Sayers of Great Yarmouth (1748–1823). (*Norfolk Museums Service*)

Norfolk worked its land as in this Norman carving on the font at St Mary's church, Burnham Deepdale. (*Photo: Peter Burton/ Harland Walshaw*)

Before machines replaced men; harvesting at Shammer, near North Creake, c.1905. (*Photo: Norfolk Rural Life Museum*)

'The Treasures of Oxnead' – painted by an unknown
seventeenth-century Dutch artist – symbolises the transient power
of the Paston family and their house. (*Norfolk Museums Service*)

The quay at Great Yarmouth in 1823 – painted by George
Vincent (1796–1832) – had lost its charm by the twentieth
century. (*Norfolk Museums Service*)

Against eighteenth century invaders: Lord Townshend reviewing
the Western Battalion of the Norfolk Militia. (*By kind permission
of the Marquess Townshend*)

Two centuries later: The Royal Norfolk Regiment inspected by
King George VI at Norwich in 1940 before sailing for Singapore
and the horrors of Japanese prison camps. (*Imperial War
Museum*)

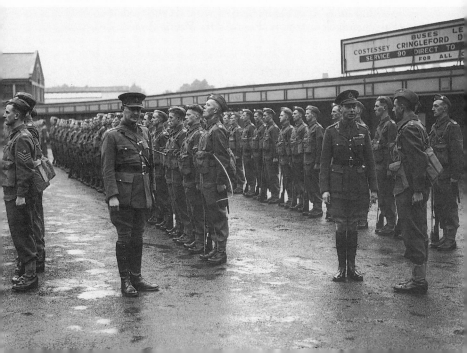

PORTRAIT 1) Norfolk reformer: Elizabeth Fry; painted in 1844 by George Richmond (1809–96). (*By kind permission of Lord Buxton*)

PORTRAIT 2) Norfolk seaman: Coxswain Henry Blogg of Cromer; painted in 1943 by Thomas Dugdale (1880–1952). (*Cromer Town Council*)

PORTRAIT 3) Norfolk gardener: Albert Corbett of Didlington Hall, photographed c.1912; he died of wounds suffered at Passchendaele in 1917. (*Photo: Mrs Maisie Gee*)

scenery around it to make amends for the town itself . . . the mediocre buildings and boot-piercing streets.'

Others saw it very differently for, by the end of the eighteenth century, the cult of the picturesque and the romantic was in place. One of the more extravagant travel-writers, Samuel Pratt, reached for his most empurpled prose to describe 'Cromer, on the trembling verge of the imperious main'. He continued,

> Had Neptune himself sent his azure chariot to receive, with a chosen suite of his Sea-Nymphs, to invite and escort me to his coral palace, I scarce could have been more awed, more softened, or more enchanted; sometimes at the window, sometimes ruminating on the cliff and sometimes pacing along, or listening to the surf-sound, the flap of the boat-sail, or the measured dash of the distant oar. My heart warmed, its sensibility kindled, its rapture glowed!

By the end of the century, lodging-houses catered for genteel visitors. 'Bathing-machines' – covered carts hauled into the edge of the sea by horses so that voluminously-suited bathers could descend steps beneath canvas hoods – were trundled into the surf; a procedure advertised as 'entirely upon new construction by which bathers are conveyed into and out of the water with Ease, Safety and Expedition'. Observers of the social scene, including the novelist Jane Austen, mentioned Cromer as a genteel resort. Its patrons were not aristocratic but drawn from the various and mutually exclusive grades of the middle class.

'The class of person which generally frequent Cromer with few exceptions is not of the highest order,' noted a cor-respondent of *Bell's Court and Fashionable Magazine* in 1807.

> It is here that the Norwich manufacturer, who has made his fortune during the war, takes up his summer retreat and exhibits all the pride and petulance of the counting-house with the insolence of new-gotten wealth . . . The next class of company . . . are the landed gentlemen of the county . . . They mingle with none but themselves; a man must have a sufficient attestation of his acres and his woods to obtain . . . an introduction to them. They repel all advances with a chill and jealous reserve peculiar to themselves.

There were no hotels as such. But the same magazine

published an account that has echoes of more recent times. 'The accommodation for company in this place is of a very humble kind,' it ran.

> Some of the fishermen have been ejected from their old cotts, or have surrendered them to a speculating bricklayer, who has spruced them up with a little fresh lath and plaster, a layer or two of sea-stone and pebbles and scrawled 'Lodgings to Let' over the window. A chandler and a jobbing carpenter have occasionally leagued together to furnish a room looking towards the sea with a few chairs, a table and a sofa; a few ale-houses, which not many years ago found it difficult from the penury of the trade to obtain a licence, or a livelihood, are now shot up into hotels and taverns; and a master of a fishing boat, a retailer of crabs, has now become the proprietor of a bathing-machine.

Cromer prospered and its landladies regularly filled their lodging-houses with visitors. But it was still a simple place. 'Cromer, always about fifty years behind other places, was at a deadlock – few lodgings (all full), no gas, no pavements', noted one visitor in 1864. Then the first hotels, designed as such, were built; the old jetty, washed away by a storm, was replaced by a simple pier; brass bands played on the esplanade. Then, in 1877, the railway reached Cromer, connecting it with Norwich and to Liverpool Street Station in London.

Now the town would occasionally be touched by the foreign and the exotic, as when the Empress Eugénie, the widow of Napoleon III, stayed there; still a militant Bonapartist she feared poisoning so insisted on seeing her breakfast milk being milked from a cow beneath her window every morning.

In the summer of 1883, a visitor arrived among the family parties on the London train, who was to transform the character of Cromer and its coast. He was Clement Scott, a journalist and theatre critic, and he planned to spend a few nights in a Cromer lodging-house. But he had not booked a room and the town was full; unable to find a bed for the night, he decided to leave his bag at the station and go for a walk along the cliffs before leaving.

Scott headed east on the footpath running along the top of the crumbling cliffs to the lighthouse and beyond. As soon as the tall tower of Cromer church was lost to view behind him, a change overcame the countryside. 'It is difficult to convey the idea of the silence of the fields through which I passed, or the beauty of the prospect that surrounded me,' he wrote later. 'A blue sky without a cloud across it; a sea sparkling under a haze of heat; wild flowers in profusion around me, poppies predominating everywhere . . . I could scarcely believe that I was only parted by a dip of coastline from music and laughter and seaside merriment, from bands and bathing-machines, from croquet and circulating libraries.'

At the edge of the cliff he saw a ruined church tower and overgrown gravestones, which touched his Victorian senti-mentality; then, a windmill on a knoll, and, below it, what was obviously the miller's house surrounded by flower-beds, 'the exact reproduction of the style of cottage that all children are set to draw when they commence their first lesson'. He knocked and asked the girl who opened the door if she took in lodgers. She did and the myth of Poppyland was born.

This was the escape from metropolitan bustle and grime of which he had dreamed in Fleet Street. So, of course, had countless others, particularly those touched by the mild, artistic bohemianism fashionable among the middle classes. So when he wrote a rapturous article about his expedition in the *Daily Telegraph* and followed it with a shamelessly sentimental poem about the forgotten graveyard, 'The Garden of Sleep' – 'On the grass of the cliff, at the edge of the steep/ God planted a garden – a garden of sleep!' – those reading it in stuffy London offices and drawing-rooms longed to take the train to Cromer and to explore what Clement Scott had named 'Poppyland'.

The miller's house had been at Sidestrand but the neigh-bouring village of Overstrand was larger, with more rooms for visitors, and it was there that seekers after tranquillity chose to settle, first in lodgings and then in their own increasingly grand holiday houses. It was not enough to order a redbrick and barge-board villa from the suburban builders' pattern books. The most fashionable young architect of the time, Edwin Lutyens (later knighted) was brought in by the rich brewer Lord Battersea to enlarge two seaside villas into an enormous architectural pantechnicon – decorated with tower, cloisters and Moorish lanterns – called The Pleasaunce; then by Lord Hillingdon to build a magnificent mock-medieval mansion more conventionally named Overstrand Hall. While at it, Lutyens built a little Methodist chapel with a lunette clerestory at Overstrand and probably had a hand in building Peartree Cottage (complete with billiards room) for Mr and Mrs Winston Churchill's summer holidays.

Cromer itself, with its railway station, was the capital of Poppyland. There the architects and builders spread themselves with new hotels and villas lining wide, leafy suburban streets. Norfolk's answer to Lutyens, George Skipper, the Norfolk architect who designed the Norwich Union office and the Royal Arcade in Norwich and Sennowe Park, built two huge, florid, redbrick hotels, the Metropole and the Hotel de Paris, to heave their bulk above the rooftops of the little town; they were kept company by others, including the Grand and the Marlborough.

The fashion for grand hotels spread west to Sheringham, a smaller version of Cromer, also a seaport with fishing boats drawn up on the beach, unloading not only crabs and lobsters but herring, cod, skate and whiting. The railway reached Sheringham a decade later than Cromer and then it was only the Midland and Great Northern Railways, which arrived from Norwich and King's Lynn via the junction at Melton Constable. It was not until 1906 that it was connected with Cromer and thence directly with the capital. Thereafter Sheringham developed a split personality. Upper Sheringham, on the wooded slopes near Humphry Repton's park around Sheringham Hall, remained a sleepy agricultural village, while Lower Sheringham imitated Cromer with hotels, lodging-houses and holiday homes.

Two other major seaside resorts grew up. The first was Hunstanton. The Le Strange family of Hunstanton Hall lived just inland of what came to be called Old Hunstanton and decided to exploit the growing demand for seaside holidays by turning Hunstanton St Edmund, on the low cliffs at the angle of the Wash and the long sweep of the Norfolk coast, into New

Hunstanton. The key to this was the arrival of the railway, after an almost straight run from London through Cambridge and Ely, in 1862. Three years later a church was built, followed by a pier, followed by a whole town, much of it designed by William Butterfield and built in the soft ginger carrstone of the region.

With its magnificent beach of hard sand and striped chalk and carrstone cliffs, New Hunstanton became fashionable not only for genteel holidays, but for preparatory schools and the infrastructure needed by visiting middle-class parents, notably the Sandringham Hotel. 'A compact little watering-place with everything on a miniature scale – a little railway station, six or seven bathing machines, etc.', wrote a visiting Norfolk clergyman on his diary in 1864, then noting that the royal seal of approval had been bestowed by the future King Edward VII on excursions from his newly-acquired country house in Sandringham. 'The most curious thing about this place is the celebrated cliff, so full of interest to the geologist. Here it is that the Prince and Princess of Wales are in the habit of taking luncheon, a servant laying the cloth on one of the rocks, while the future King of England sits on another, smoking his cigar.'

There were, of course, other resorts and some of them catered for visitors with other tastes. Great Yarmouth had made the most of its long, sandy beach and offered more robust entertainment for crowds from nearby Norwich and, as cheap hotels and boarding-houses opened, from London and the Midlands: Punch and Judy shows, 'nigger minstrels', beauty and 'knobby knees' competitions. Here, in 1859, the same observant parson found that 'Yarmouth is immensely improved by a splendid Marine Drive some two miles long, facing the sands and lighted with gas. It has altered the place completely.'

The coast between the three working seaports and the four resorts remained undisturbed until the end of the First World War. Perhaps in reaction to this and to the horrors of that war, which were felt in every Norfolk village, there was a surge of longing for loneliness and rural peace, a return to Poppyland. Bird-watching spread beyond the ornithologist, and nature reserves – particularly those on Scolt Head Island and Blakeney Point – and a coast that had been regarded as a desolate wasteland, good only for wildfowling and mussel-gathering, acquired a new significance.

The attraction of this lonely shore was described by Miss E. L. Turner, who, in 1924, became the first official 'watcher' on Scolt Head, in her book, published four years later, *Bird-Watching on Scolt Head*. She wrote,

> The island with its long backbone of sandhills, flanked by the sea on the north and wide salt-marshes on the south, possesses beauty both of form and colour. One never tired of watching the wind tossing the tawny manes of the marram grass and driving the great galleon-like clouds across the sky, or chasing their shadows over the wet sand. The gradual changes which almost imperceptibly crept over the mud flats were a revelation to me. In early April they looked uniformly dun-coloured unless touched up by sunset or sunrise. But as the stately pageant of summer passed by, each month brought its own flowers and revealed new beauties . . . grey and gold, orange and scarlet, copper and brown, while the tide filled the runnels with blue and silver. The great salt marsh . . . was like a vast oriental carpet spread at one's feet.'

The habits of the sea birds – the terns, oyster-catchers, waders and the great flocks of migratory birds – beguiled visitors. Villagers on the coast found their knowledge and guidance in demand and several families of reserve wardens and boatmen became recognised authorities; at Scolt Head, the Chesneys, father and son, both wardens; the Haines, father and son, both named Bill, watermen and ornithologists. Bird-watching was popularised in the 1930s when the artist Peter Scott began painting wildfowl over the East Anglian salt-marshes, and his prints of ducks against a wide sky decorated many a middle-class drawing-room.

Sailing, long a minority sport, became more popular with the introduction of sailing boats in recognised classes, which could be raced on the Broads and in the estuaries and harbours at Brancaster Staithe, Burnham Overy Staithe, Morston and Blakeney, the first and last of these becoming holiday destinations with a golf course along the dunes at Brancaster and a smart hotel at Blakeney. Caravan parks and shanty-towns of beach-huts, bungalows and even wheel-less railway carriages appeared in the coastal dunes. It was only after the Second World War that some order was introduced to such human habitats. The National Trust and the conservancy organisations combined with local authority to sweep away the haphazard development and corral the caravans, albeit in even bigger concentrations.

But the increase in desirability of the coast prompted an influx of prosperous city-dwellers from London and the Midlands to buy second homes there. A few such had been cottage-owners since the Twenties and Thirties – sometimes Cambridge dons – but in the prosperous Sixties there was a rush for weekend escape and, within twenty years, new arrivals became the majority in the prettier coastal villages. Overy Creek, a harbour for sailing coasters within living memory, had silted up but still allowed small-boat sailing, so that in the middle years of the century, wooden, clinker- or carvel-built dinghies raced; two decades later, well-to-do townspeople with holiday cottages (sometimes holiday manor houses and old rectories) sailed their fibreglass catamarans and shot across the water on windsurfing boards.

Those preferring less demanding aquatic activity chose the Broads, which cover 220 square miles with reed-bordered meres and channels linking the rivers of east Norfolk and the sea. Yet they have become so choked with pleasure boats – more than 12,000 at the last count, nine-tenths of them powered by petrol or diesel oil – that pollution from leaked fuel and sewage is fast destroying both their beauty and their ecology. Indeed, in 1983, the University of East Anglia reported to the Countryside Commission that thirty of the fifty-two lakes in Broadland had had their ecology destroyed by the combination of pollution from these craft and the leaching of chemical fertilisers from the surrounding farmland and that only four could still support the fish, plants and birds that once thrived in these placid lagoons.

Those English holidaymakers who would rather gaze at the sea than venture upon it divided themselves, as is their way, into categories. Those who enjoyed the pleasures of the urban seaside chose the little resorts of Hunstanton,

Sheringham or Cromer with their boarding-houses and fish teas (all three somewhat *déclassé* by the second half of the twentieth century); for cheerful open-air communal living, there were vast caravan sites, notably along the flat shores south of Mundesley; for exuberance touched with traditional seaside vulgarity there was Great Yarmouth with esplanade and funfair raucous with amplified pop music and sticky with candyfloss.

But the English middle class tended to opt for mock-pastoral sojourns in villages on, or within easy reach of, the coast. Hotels and boarding-houses were few so they tended to rent, or buy, cottages, which had been built a century or two before for fishermen and farm workers.

So the villages themselves have changed in character, if not in looks, beyond recognition. On weekdays in winter, night falls on darkened cottages, awaiting their latest occupants, perhaps on Friday night, but more likely at Easter, while the surviving villagers are left with their memories of an extinct community that had filled its church and school. Village shops close and, in the market towns, shops open to cater for the visitors, who brought with them new ideas in fashion and furniture for country living. In Burnham Market, once a robust village of pubs, butchers and bakers and a grocer, who sold waterboots and hams as well as peppercorns and baked beans, there flourish antique shops, fashion boutiques, a bookshop offering the latest novels, assorted gift shops and a sophisticated delicatessen. Like all migrations, this has had both bad effects and some good ones, too: new initiatives, businesses and enthusiasm for preserving the peace which attracted the incomers.

Although deep-sea ships never sailed from Norfolk ports, they and the coast's creeks and estuaries became the nursery of great seafarers. Sadly, few of the names of the earliest seafarers are recorded; possibly some of the Viking settlers had voyaged to Iceland, or had crossed the Atlantic. But one of the first to be remembered by name is one of the most romantic: John Rolfe (1585–1622) of Heacham Hall, a West Norfolk landowner. He and his young wife had sailed in a fleet of migrants to try to extend their fortune in Virginia but were shipwrecked and finally landed at their destination in 1610 from boats made from their ship's timbers. Life in America was a struggle against disease and hostile Indians but Rolfe managed to cultivate tobacco and emerged as a leader of his settlement. His wife died but then he met the daughter of an Indian chief, who was being held hostage against the behaviour of her tribe, although she was popular with the settlers for having saved the life of the leader of the Jamestown settlement, Captain John Smith, who had been about to be murdered by Indians four years before. Her name was Pocahontas (1595–1617).

John Rolfe fell in love with the Indian girl, converted her to Christianity, married her and re-named her Rebecca. In 1616, he brought her and their infant son to England, where, dressed in high Tudor fashion, she was presented to the King and Queen but soon fell victim to the climate and her health began to suffer. Rolfe decided that they should return to Virginia but at the beginning of the journey, while waiting at Gravesend on the Thames to board a ship of Sir Walter Raleigh's last trans-Atlantic expedition lying in the Thames, she died. Her son, however, was to father a notable American line of descent, while his mother is remembered by a statue at Gravesend and a fine modern bust in alabaster in Heacham church.

Thereafter, the most celebrated Norfolk sailors made their reputations with the Navy. Indeed four famous admirals – Myngs, Narborough, Shovell and the great Nelson himself – came from the twenty-mile stretch of coast between Burnham Overy Staithe and Salthouse where the creeks wind through salt-marshes and sand dunes to the sea.

Vice-Admiral Sir Christopher Myngs (1625–66) was born at Salthouse in 1625. He served at sea under Prince Rupert and proved a successful admiral in the Dutch wars. He fought in the Battle of Lowestoft (an English victory) in 1665 and in the Four Days Battle a year later. This was a victory for the Dutch, and Myngs himself was mortally wounded on the quarterdeck of his flagship, the *Victory*, never living to see the reversal of English fortunes at the Battle of Orfordness soon after. He was popular: his ship's company volunteering to man a fireship to attack the Dutch and avenge his death and Samuel Pepys noting that he had been 'a man of great parts and most excellent tongue'.

Rear-Admiral Sir John Narborough (1640–88) was born at Cockthorpe near Salthouse in 1640 and first went to sea as Myngs' servant (the usual means of training to become a naval officer was to be rated as such, or as a volunteer, or able seaman, before being promoted to midshipman). He, too, fought the Dutch and was with Myngs when he was killed, thereafter serving in the West Indies and the Mediterranean before joining the Board of Admiralty. He died on an abortive treasure-hunt in the Caribbean, where he was buried and his internal organs sent home, pickled, for burial. While a captain, he, too, had taken another Norfolk boy, Cloudesley Shovell, also from Cockthorpe, on board his ship as a servant.

This boy became Vice-Admiral Sir Cloudesley Shovell (1650–1707), who made his name at sea in the late seventeenth and early eighteenth centuries, commanding a squadron at the capture of Gibraltar. After commanding the Mediterranean Fleet, Admiral Shovell was returning to England in 1707, when his flagship and three other ships were wrecked on the Scilly Islands. Shovell was washed ashore, his bulky body found half-drowned on the beach by a woman, who, seeing the emerald ring on his finger, pressed his face into the wet sand until he suffocated, and then stole the ring. Sadly, he often seems a grotesque, rather comic figure – perhaps because of his odd name and the manner of his death – until one comes upon his portrait bust in the Stranger's Hall at Norwich. There he is in the periwig and stock of his day, but the face is arresting and looks contemporary: a tough, humorous face; a face accustomed to both command and enjoyment; a face one seems to know, and the sight of it brings a twinge of anger at his fate.

Captain George Vancouver (1757–98) was born at King's Lynn, sailed as a boy with Captain Cook, and himself became a celebrated navigator and explorer. He gave his name, of course, to the Canadian city and, along that remote coast, Norfolk names to the Lynn Channel and Holkham Bay, and he named ports after Snettisham, Houghton, Coke and Windham. One of the great navigators in the great age of navigation, Vancouver is remembered for his surveys of the North American coast but he also surveyed the south-west shores of Australia and sailed the unknown waters of the Pacific. A hard-driving disciplinarian, Vancouver was worn out by the age of thirty-eight and returned home to edit his journals, a task which was completed by his brother. He died at Petersham, a charming village on the placid Thames near Richmond, in 1798 and is buried there.

Horatio Nelson (1758–1805) was born a year after Vancouver at Burnham Thorpe. He was to become the greatest British hero – perhaps the first truly popular national hero – his two cataclysmic victories in Aboukir Bay and off Cape Trafalgar destroying Napoleon's ambitions beyond the Continent and giving his country maritime supremacy and peace for a century.

Nelson was a distinct product of his environment. He was a Norfolkman in his independence of mind and his distrust of foreigners, albeit those overseas rather than, as was, and sometimes is, the case with Norfolk people, from the next county. His social position framed his attitudes. His father's family was educated middle-class; clergymen and the occasional tradesman (his paternal grandmother was a baker's daughter from Cambridge). But his mother belonged to a 'county' family, the Sucklings, who were related to other landowning Norfolk families, notably the Walpoles of Houghton and Wolterton. Bearing a less imposing name than his mother's may have added an edge of social insecurity for he was constantly reminded of this: while he and his wife occasionally stayed with his distant cousin Lord Walpole at Wolterton Hall they were never invited to the grander Houghton Hall.

One of his brothers, Suckling Nelson, was a failure as a village shopkeeper. It is odd to read a letter from Nelson about visiting his brother: 'I was at Elmham yesterday and your cloth was packed up but my brother waited till he got down the Blue for turnups and lining . . . ' Two of his sisters worked as shop assistants and he had social aspirations for his favourite sister Kate; his sister Susannah had married into the Bolton family, prosperous merchants at Wells-next-the-Sea, and he wrote: 'Although I am very fond of Mrs. Bolton, I own I should not like to see my little Kate fixed in a Wells society'; he did not have to for she married the dashing George Matcham and lived for a time at Barton Hall, a smart house in the east of the county.

Then, as in the next century, the taking of Holy Orders was a means of social advancement. At the time, the status of the parson was above that of the lawyer and the doctor. Some were related to the aristocracy and those of more ordinary origins could join the grandees if, for example, they could make a mark on the hunting field, at cards, politics or even offer amusing company in the scattered, often dull, society of the countryside. But all were aware that the grandest of the landowners was, in the end, likely to come to them to ask for intercession with their Maker, with whom they were assumed to enjoy privileged communion. Thus Nelson, who numbered more than a dozen parsons among his relations and immediate forebears, would have had a strong, sub-conscious sense of spiritual privilege and so self-confidence.

His mother's death when he was at the vulnerable age of nine left him in the care of village women when not away at school at Norwich and then at North Walsham. His liking for them and his sympathy for the poverty of their families gave him an understanding of the farm labourers and, later, of seamen that was part of the secret of his brilliance as a commander. He was loved by his men and it was easy to understand why. Visiting wounded sailors in hospital at Great Yarmouth after the Battle of Copenhagen he noticed a young man who, like himself, had lost his right arm. 'Why, Jack!' he said, 'you and I are spoiled for fishermen.'

When Nelson returned to sea for his twelve years of mounting fame, he took with him several Norfolk boys as 'captain's servants' to be trained as officers. Amongst them were the sons of the rectors of Rollesby (Billy Bolton, related by marriage to his sister Susannah) and Sedgeford (handsome

Thomas Weatherhead, who, before he was killed in action at Tenerife, was to be described as 'the darling of the ship's company'), and William Hoste, the keen young son of the rector of Tittleshall. His servant, Tom Allen, was one of the men he took with him from the Burnhams to serve as seamen; he proved a true Norfolkman and when, on arrival at Naples, King Ferdinand came aboard the flagship and extended a hand to be kissed, Allen shook it, saying 'How d'ye do, Mr King'.

Nelson said that he gloried in being a Norfolkman and spoke of 'dear, dear Burnham', associating it with the happy days of childhood before the death of his mother. 'The thought of former days,' he once wrote, 'brings all my mother to my heart, which shows itself in my eyes.' He never returned to Burnham Thorpe after his recall to sea in February 1793, even for his father's funeral there – although he made detailed arrangements for it by letter – because he feared he might meet his estranged wife at the graveside. So his only visits were to Great Yarmouth, when returning from the Mediterranean with the Hamiltons in 1800, when sailing for the Baltic a year later and on his return.

But Norfolk kept in touch with him and his mounting fame. Not only were his victories celebrated with parades, dinners and dances but pubs were named after him throughout the county: 'The Lord Nelson', 'The Norfolk Hero' or just 'The Hero', for there was only one hero worthy of the description. To this day, the church of All Saints at Burnham Thorpe flies from its tower a replica of the flag Nelson flew at the Battle of the Nile on the anniversary of his death at Trafalgar on 21 October 1805.

Nelson's favourite protégé and professional heir was William Hoste (1780–1828), the parson's son from Godwick Hall, near Tittleshall. They served together until after the Battle of the Nile when the latter was given his own command. When Nelson was killed, Hoste became a brilliant frigate captain, and an inspiration for the character of Hornblower in C. S. Forester's historical novels. Hoste captured the supposedly impregnable fortress-cities of Ragusa (now Dubrovnik) and Cattaro (now Kotor) by hauling his ship's guns to the summits of commanding mountains and, as it were, bombarding them from the air. He fought and won a Trafalgar in miniature in an action between frigate squadrons in the Adriatic at the Battle of Lissa, when, just before opening fire, he made the signal, 'Remember Nelson'.

William Hoste's reward was a baronetcy and large amounts of prize-money, which continued long after the end of the war as prize courts ground through the backlog of claims. Yet most of that seems to have been spent by his father, the Revd Dixon Hoste, on electioneering for his friend Thomas Coke (a Whig politician as well as an agricultural pioneer) in the hope of a bishopric. William loaned his father thousands of pounds and, in 1813, wrote to him from the Adriatic, 'It grieves me to find that my Father should deceive me, that *even the interest* of the Money I came forward with two years ago should not be paid, how then can the Principal?'

Like his hero, Hoste hankered after Norfolk and his home, 'dear old Godwick'. The Tudor house, Godwick Hall – formerly the home of the Cokes before they moved to Holkham – stood in uneven fields, which showed it to be the site of an abandoned village, across the fields from Tittleshall (later it fell into neglect and its ruins were demolished in the 1950s). Often in letters home from the Mediterranean and Adriatic he would describe the convivial scenes he imagined around the dining-room table and, after a long absence, mused, 'I think I could find my way from Tittleshall to Godwick, but no further'. From Florence, he wrote, 'I have been at the famous Sculptor's yesterday and I purchased some beautiful figures in Alabaster, which I intend for the dear old house in Norfolk'. He was generous to his own men and, when commanding the brig *Mutine* in the Mediterranean, was delighted to hear that some of the Norfolkmen, recruited by Nelson and who had been wounded, had found their way home and called on his parents. He wrote,

The sailor you were good enough to take care of did belong to the *Mutine* . . . Poor fellow! he lost his arm, as he told you, in cutting out some vessels on the Italian coast. Should you see him again, give him a good dinner on my account; for, though he did not bear the best character with me, yet he was as brave as a lion and behaved very well in the fighting way.

He nurtured a fierce local patriotism and was outraged on meeting a Captain Langford from King's Lynn, where he had clearly felt socially insecure. Writing that they had had 'a good deal of talk, or *gab* together', including 'a good deal of old Norfolk', he was horrified to discover that Langford 'abominates the very *mention* of the County, he says everybody is so cursed proud and *unsociable* that he was heartily glad to cut and run'. This was too much for Hoste, who 'stuck out most sturdily for the *honour* of Norfolk' and 'gave it the preference to any other county in England and rather too boldly asserted that the *fine flat variegated* scenery, particularly around Swaffham and Brandon, was equal to the so-much-boasted garden of Kent, or the *beautiful romantic* hill and dale of Westmorland and Lancashire'. Hoste lived to command the royal yacht for King William IV, the 'Sailor King', but followed Vancouver into retirement at Petersham and died of tuberculosis at the age of forty-eight.

Not all the county's naval notables were seafarers. Sir Robert Seppings (1767–1840) had a profound impact on British sea power but rarely went to sea. Born at Fakenham, he was apprenticed to the naval dockyard at Plymouth, where he invented a system of supporting hulls in dry-dock as result of which he was appointed master shipwright at Chatham. It was there, at the time of Trafalgar, that he became aware of the inherent weaknesses of traditional warship design both in storm and in battle. In heavy seas, ships could 'hog', or break their backs, through longitudinal weaknesses and in action their decks could be raked by an enemy firing through the weak structure of the bows, or through the great array of windows at the stern. He therefore proposed two innovations: one, inspired by the structure of the Norfolk five-barred gate with the diagonal brace, was that hulls should be strengthened with such diagonal beams; the other, that the main structure of the hull should be rounded at bow and stern, the latter losing its familiar tiers of windows but being protected by thick timber pierced for gun-ports, so increasing the number of guns that could be mounted. Towards the end of the wars, Seppings became Surveyor of the Navy, was then knighted and finally faded from the public consciousness, to be remembered briefly when, in one of those curious cross-references of history, his son was killed in the massacre of Cawnpore in the Indian Mutiny.

The great age of naval heroes might seem to be past, but Nelson and Hoste were to be followed by some worthy heirs. It was a Norfolkman, Lieutenant Gurney Cresswell (1827–67) of King's Lynn, who made the final link in the discovery of the North-West Passage across the top of North America. In 1845, Captain Sir John Franklin had sailed with his two ships, the *Erebus* and *Terror*, in an attempt to discover what might prove to be an alternative to the dangerous passage of Cape Horn to reach the Pacific westabout. The ships and their crews were never heard of again and not seen until the frozen body of one of Franklin's men was discovered in its shallow grave nearly a century and a half later. Amongst a number of expeditions sent to find Franklin was that of the *Enterprise* and *Investigator*, which set out in 1850 to search the western end of the supposed channel. In October that year, Lieutenant Cresswell and a small landing party waded through deep snow to the summit of the 1,400-foot mountain on Victoria Island and then saw to the east a great sheet of ice. From its position Cresswell knew that this was what had been named Melville Sound when it had first been seen, three decades earlier, by Captain (later Rear-Admiral) Sir William Parry, who had approached it *from the opposite direction*. That view from the summit showed that this was the North-West Passage, or it would be were it not choked with ice. It was not for nearly three years that Cresswell returned to England, bringing with him the first news of the discovery, and not for another four that the first report of the disaster that had befallen Franklin was received. Cresswell continued his career in the China Sea, hunting pirates, and was promoted to captain but, on his return to King's Lynn, he died aged only thirty.

More fortunate was another Victorian naval officer, Admiral of the Fleet Arthur Knyvet Wilson (1842–1921);

born at Swaffham thirty-seven years after the death of Nelson, he first served in his former flagship, the *Victory*. His own fame was not won at sea but while fighting ashore with the Naval Brigade in the Sudan in 1884. After retirement as an admiral in 1912, he was recalled to succeed Admiral of the Fleet Lord Fisher (1841–1920) as First Sea Lord in 1915. While his great predecessor joined the pantheon of naval history, Wilson retired to Swaffham where he helped design the war memorial and the golf course. The other Victorian, Lord Fisher, owned a magnificent house, Kilverstone Hall, near Thetford, and his title was Baron Fisher of Kilverstone but he cannot be considered a Norfolkman. Indeed, he acquired his estate in a way that would, to say the least, have raised eyebrows a century later. Admiral Fisher, who introduced the revolutionary *Dreadnought* class of battleships armed only with heavy guns, was a great innovator and, when Director of Naval Ordnance in the 1880s, struck up a professional friendship with William Vavasseur, the technical director of the armaments manufacturer, Armstrong. Vavasseur, the owner of Kilverstone, was so taken with Fisher that he left his estate and fortune to his son Cecil, making him his heir on condition he took his own name and this was duly added in 1909 after his benefactor's death. Meanwhile Admiral Fisher used the house and its three thousand acres as his own – he even set up the figurehead of his first ship, the *Calcutta*, in the garden – and entertained lavishly, his shooting parties expecting a daily bag of at least a thousand pheasants. He had his crest of a mailed fist clutching a trident carved on his gateposts and he and his wife were buried in the churchyard. But, although he had been nominated for his naval cadetship by the last of Nelson's captains and himself became the most vital and innovative naval officer since Nelson, the parallels did not include the territorial, for Fisher was only, as it were, mooring in Norfolk at the end of a long and stormy life.

Yet there is another link with the county, albeit one that does him and his reputation no credit. On the outbreak of war in 1914, the First Lord of the Admiralty, Winston Churchill, recalled Fisher to be First Sea Lord, the appointment from which he had retired four years earlier, and it was then that, against his better judgement, he had supported Churchill's scheme for an attack on the Dardanelles; when it failed, he resigned. Had Fisher been true to his strategic and, once the campaign had begun, his tactical convictions, the 5th Norfolks would not have vanished into that burning wood on the heights of Gallipoli.

Not all of those returning from service with the Royal Navy were celebrated admirals and captains. During the Napoleonic wars, a traveller in south-west Norfolk was approached by a discharged sailor, Tom Cox, late of HMS *Diomede*, who asked, 'Master, will you tell a lame fellow how far it is to Lynn? I have limped all the way with this bundle in my hand from Plymouth, where I have been invalided and laid up as idle as a hulk these four months; and I am now going to the hammock of a friend at Lynn.'

A full-blooded Norfolkman from Burnham Norton, Richard Woodget (1847–1928) was one of the last great captains of sail. His seafaring was in merchantmen, and his most famous ship was the clipper *Cutty Sark*, which he commanded for a decade from 1885. The speed of the clippers bringing wool, or tea home from Australia and China was legendary; they made the passage to Australia in 170 days and back in 80, sometimes proving faster than the new steam passenger liners. The seas he described in his log were a long way from the Norfolk creeks he loved. 'An immense sea rolled up right aft,' he recorded in 1891. 'When I looked at it, towering up so steep, in fact, like a cliff, it looked as if it were about to drop down over our stern and completely bury the ship.' It did. 'It dropped on board with tremendous force,' he continued. 'The water was up to my waist whilst I was hanging on the rail; you could see nothing but the boats and the masts, the whole ship was completely submerged . . . During the 31 years I have been sailing the seas, I never saw anything approaching it in size and steepness.'

Like many clipper captains, Woodget had his eccentricities, amongst which was his hobby, which he insisted his apprentices share, of roller-skating around the deck of the ship on calmer days at sea. He also bred collie dogs and took them to sea; when his favourite, Lassie, died he had her stuffed and kept her in the hall of his house ashore so that he could pat her as he passed. Woodget was a tough, efficient man, whether driving his crews to make even better times on long voyages or, latterly, running a small mixed farm in Norfolk. His famous ship survived to dock finally, in 1953, at Greenwich, where she still lies, and Captain Woodget retired to Burnham Overy Staithe, his blunt, weathered face framed by white, bristly hair. There, he named his first cottage after a Sydney anchorage, *Warrawee*, and liked to sail his small, clinker-built boat along the coast to Wells. One of his young neighbours remembered that, when crewing for Captain Woodget, the first sign of sudden bad weather would be when he began chewing his moustache, then singing psalms, and that he had done this once off Wells when a storm had blown out of the North Sea.

His son Harold was also a seafarer, also sailed in the *Cutty Sark* and also retired to Overy. Once, visiting the author's cottage there, historical times seemed to telescope when the old man noticed a painting of an action between British and French frigates on the wall. The old man's eyes narrowed in the hard, high-cheekboned face and, as one of his ancestors might have said in Nelson's time, he exclaimed, 'The French flag!'

One of the few Norfolk seafarers to achieve fame in East Anglian waters was Henry Blogg (1876–1954), coxswain of the Cromer lifeboat, which he joined in 1894 when he was eighteen. During the next half-century his lifeboat saved nearly 900 lives and Coxswain Blogg was decorated with the George Cross and five other medals for skill and courage at sea; he looked the part with his strong, humorous face, beaming underneath a yellow oilskin sou'wester. Surprisingly, perhaps, he neither drank nor smoked and never learned to swim. Once, when a visitor to Cromer stood beside him watching great breakers bursting along the beach and remarked on the beauty of the sea, he replied in his broad Norfolk accent, 'No, my dear. That ent bewtiful, thass cruel.' When he died in 1954, the latest, but perhaps not quite the last, of an aquatic breed of men, three thousand mourners attended his funeral.

Other retired seafarers settled into the Norfolk countryside. For example, close to the former homes of Nelson and Woodget, came Vice-Admiral Sir Hector MacLean (b. 1908), who navigated the destroyer *Cossack* up a Norwegian fjord in 1940 to board the German ship *Altmark* in the celebrated action that rescued more that 300 British merchant seamen imprisoned aboard. There was Mark Cheyne (b. 1910), who left Ditchingham, the home of his famous grandfather Sir Rider Haggard, to win the Distinguished Service Cross in a night action between destroyers in the Mediterranean. There were many such men of character, slipping into village life and often taking command of it.

In coastal villages families of seafarers and watermen, engaged in ferrying holidaymakers, gathering mussels, fishing for crab, lobster and mackerel, founded rival dynasties. Typical, perhaps, was Burnham Overy Staithe with its three families —Haines, Lane and Thompson — each with their devoted admirers among the holiday people. The patriarchs were Billy Haines with his curly hair and blue eyes, who had rescued British soldiers from the beaches of Dunkirk; Laddie Lane, who had rowed other British soldiers across the Tigris under fire in the earlier world war; Welcome Thompson, a barrel-shaped man in yellow oilskins. Such men became part of the childhood legends of those they ferried down to the gloriously empty sands.

Of Billy Haines, the poet Kevin Crossley-Holland, who spent holidays in Overy, wrote,

> He knows these creeks, inch by inch,
> their silt and shining, their dark complexities,
> and when to shoulder the *Rosemary* into action,
> veterans both of Dunkirk.
>
> 'C'mon, then, me bootie!'
> Infirm and elderly and eager young
> he hands from jetty into bows,
> a salt shepherd
> gentling doubts, winking at such high hopes.

Billy's son served in the Royal Navy, then took his father's place at the tiller of their boat in Overy Creek.

Conscription in wartime – with National Service for two decades after the Second World War – had, of course, replaced the press gang but, as in Nelson's time, there were always volunteers and, instead of the boys from poor backgrounds being sent to sea by the Marine Society, there was the Watts Naval Training School. This was the old County School, bought by the shipowner E. H. Watts in 1902 for sea-training and, for most of the time until it closed in 1949, administered by Dr Barnardo's Homes. My father was a Governor and, as a child from London, I remember the Watts boys of my own age with their cropped hair and bright, alert eyes. Thousands went to sea from that hill-top school outside North Elmham and there cannot have been a major naval engagement in either world war in which it was not represented.

Except for the flotillas of pleasure boats that swarmed from its creeks in summer, East Anglia became far less involved with the sea in the second half of the twentieth century. The ports of King's Lynn and Yarmouth, and the lesser port of Wells, survived and sometimes prospered but the coastal trade was now transported by road and the fleets of fishing boats had mostly given way to the distant factory-ship.

Yet, occasionally, the old skills showed themselves, as they did again at Burnham Overy Staithe, where Nelson had first seen the sea. There lives the Beck family: the father, trained as a shipwright in the Royal Navy, managing the creek and its sailing-boat repairing and moorings, and his two sons brought up in this tradition. These two young men and a few friends spent four years building a 28-ton, ocean-going yacht, the *Overy Action*, in the yard behind their father's boathouse. Launched in 1993, she crossed the Atlantic at the end of the year, beginning a voyage round the world. Their letters and telephone calls home sounded echoes of their predecessors: they anchored in English Harbour, the West Indian 'hurricane hole' at Antigua, where Nelson had once commanded the frigates; they passed the Panama Canal, the short-cut to the

Pacific, which the disastrous expedition into Nicaragua had been designed to open and which nearly cost Nelson his life; they had crossed the Pacific, calling at the Galapagos Islands, where Darwin had studied the origins of species, often in the wake of Captain Cook, also a seaman from the east coast of England, and had been welcomed at the island of Tonga, as he had been, but at Tahiti found the French as unfriendly as maritime tradition suggested. At the boathouse in Overy, their course was plotted on a global map as the yacht, which had so recently anchored in this creek between the salt-marshes, steered through coral reefs into blue lagoons.

Norfolk still uses the sea but the sea takes its tolls. The sandy cliffs from Weybourne to Happisburgh are pounded and crumbled by the surf, and the high dunes of Scolt Head and Blakeney are swept away to become sandbanks and a hazard to shipping. The eastern coast of England is sinking as the whole island tips. Tidal surges combined with north-easterly wind, can sweep across the saltings and breast the banks, flooding the once-reclaimed fields beyond. The most lethal of these was the great flood of 1953, when dozens were drowned, but seaside villages have been flooded since, and small ships left stranded on the coast road, by the sea flexing its muscles. Oddly, the Norfolk coast has something in common with Venice to one who knows and loves both places: beauty made poignant by vulnerability.

IV
Faith

When Russell Thorndike, brother of Dame Sybil and himself an actor, retired to a de-licensed pub in Foulsham, he liked to remark that it was appropriate that he should return to his East Anglian roots. When asked to elaborate, the old story-teller – celebrated for his novels about Dr Syn, the smuggler-parson of Romney Marsh – would transfix his questioner with a round-eyed stare and declare, 'Our name, of course. We are descended from a Viking. He sprang ashore on a Norfolk beach, swinging his battleaxe and shouting his war-cry. "*Thor und ich!*" – Thor and I – and so, Thorndike.'

Since that distant time, the invocation of the Deity has been as important to the life of this county as to others and, indeed, to all countries. It may seem a far cry from the longship on the beach to Christmas Day at St Mary Magdalene, at Sandringham, but there is a direct link: the need for spiritual reassurance. This carrstone church, much restored by the Victorians, has become embedded in the British tradition. It is on the Sandringham estate and there the royal family attend services at Christmas, watched by crowds in pixie-hoods and anoraks. The Queen has already recorded her Christmas message, but her father and grandfather sat before the microphone in the library at Sandringham House to address their Empire, again invoking the Deity, albeit no longer Thor. The place and the occasion is redolent of family cosiness. When my grandfather preached here, he would stay at Sandringham House and once, presumably at this season, organised the royal family for a sing-song round a piano with the Prince of Wales strumming a banjo and Queen Mary blowing through a comb wrapped in tissue paper.

If that church symbolises the reassuring Christianity

practised by the Church of England in the late nineteenth and the twentieth centuries, then another church on the Sandringham estate recalls its roots. Just to the west of the road running north from King's Lynn, near the old railway station at Wolferton, where Christmas guests were once welcomed by courtiers in top hats waiting on a red carpet, stands a ruined church, also of carrstone. This is the church of St Felix at Babingley, named after the saint who spread Christianity in Norfolk before the first Thorndike arrived in a pagan thunderclap.

St Felix had followed St Augustine to East Anglia early in the seventh century, and had been welcomed by King Sigbert, himself baptised a Christian. St Felix was Bishop of East Anglia for seventeen years, and the first church at Babingley was said to have been built near the beach where he came ashore in the Wash at the beginning of his mission to north-west Norfolk. After St Felix's time, the See of East Anglia was split into two with cathedrals at North Elmham and Thetford. Monasteries were founded and became seats of learning; the great Christian tradition, which, despite early setbacks, has shaped society and its attitudes, was being formed. Churches were built across the county: solid, thick-walled little churches with stubby towers – like that still standing above All Saints, Newton-by-Castle Acre – sometimes built with recycled Roman bricks and with a look of village churches on the far shore of the North Sea.

There was, of course, a far older religious tradition and some of the ancient festivals were absorbed into the new church calendar. The very earliest religious instinct had probably found expression in the worship of the sun and natural phenomena.

Man's search for the meaning and a pattern for life left its first recognisable mark near Arminghall south of Norwich. This consists of no more than a circular bank in the centre of which remain holes into which uprights were once sunk. What their purpose was, none can tell, but it is assumed to have been ceremonial and probably religious. Perhaps, some early Druidical cult worshipped at sunrise here, as at Stonehenge.

With the Romans came order, in religion as in all else. Into the pagan groves of East Anglia trooped the pantheon of gods and goddesses from the Mediterranean, their marble statues pale against pale skies. The only major temple in Norfolk was at the new capital, Venta Icenorum – again near Arminghall – where a fine stone temple was built. Small Romano-British towns and settlements had their own parish temples and, of course, each Romanised family had its own stone altar to its household gods. Christianity had not arrived in England when Roman rule reached its final, formal end in AD 410 and East Anglia was left to defend itself against invasion from across the North Sea.

At first the Scandinavians, Angles and Saxons came to settle, not conquer, and, despite a resident population of several hundred thousand, there was plenty of space once woodland had been cleared for farming. It was not until the ninth century that the Danes – the Vikings – arrived with plunder in mind. At first, there was no thought of settlement and the new Christian monasteries and churches – usually at the centre of wealth and culture – were sacked and their priests slaughtered. The Norse gods also came across the sea to leave behind them the names of villages rather than temples. Thor's garden became Thurgarten and Thornham, Thornage, Thursford and Thurton are among those calling to mind the god of thunder, who seemed to displace the Christians' God of Love, albeit temporarily.

The restored power of Christianity, here as throughout the British Isles and Europe, is proclaimed by the churches which have survived the centuries and, here and there, the millennium. If such a demonstration were required, it is only necessary to look upon the vast magnificence of Norwich Cathedral, built at a time from which only the Norman castle survives in the city and, of the two, the spiritual out-classes the secular in scale and splendour.

The prime builder was Herbert de Losinga, the prior of Fécamp, who was appointed Bishop of East Anglia at the end of the eleventh century when the seat of the northern See was moved from Thetford to Norwich. His was the vision of a vast cathedral that could only receive its final consecration long after his own death. It was he who commissioned the architects and masons, several of whose names are known, and it was he who ordered Norman stone from the quarries of Caen. Thereafter there was building and rebuilding after collapse in a fire and this work continued, making the cathedral almost a living organism. The cathedral seen in the twentieth century is a harmonious mixture of the Norman and later Perpendicular styles, combining in one of the great stone buildings of Europe. The daring of the design is shown by the spire, standing 315 ft tall, which collapsed in the fourteenth century and was rebuilt again on a Norman tower not designed to support it, and now seems an integral part of the Norfolk landscape. This is more than a technological miracle, it is a finger pointing heavenward, its converging lines a symbol of eternity. If ever man's aspirations found expression, they found it here.

The Cathedral Church of the Holy and Undivided Trinity stands now as it stood then, inspiring awe with its sheer scale and beauty. Looking at it from different viewpoints, within and without, its composition will stay in the memory as a vision close to sublime. Happily, my own is the view of the interior of the tower with its supporting columns, vaults and clerestories seen from where the bronze, sculpted face of my grandfather, Bishop Bowers, smiles from his memorial in the chancel.

The hold the cathedral can exert was captured by my father in a novel* about a cathedral city (based on Norwich, where he was courting my mother and met her friends in The Close) and he described the thoughts of one of his characters, the unmarried daughter of the Dean:

> The cathedral had become part of her very make-up and being, as it had of her father's. She loved it – loved the tremendous Norman pillars, the snoring organ notes that rang vibrating round the clerestory; the lights, and the brasses, and the pottering vergers. Hours of every day of her life she spent in and about the cathedral, and she could not have told where her deep cathedral sense merged with her religion.

* *Period Programme*, (J. M. Dent) London, 1936.

Oh, but she feared it, too! It was the sense of immolation that she feared – the knowledge that she was imprisoned in that beautiful building and all it symbolized just as surely as if she had taken the veil. There were times when this fear came upon her as a sort of spiritual claustrophobia; and then she would pull herself together and hurry home to her petty duties, often with a bitter but bracing little laugh at herself.

Such is the power of this building.

Also making this urban landscape are the other churches of the city, thirty-two of them; at the end of the eleventh century, when the city had a population of 5,500, there were already twenty-one. All were once thronged and, when ruled from the Vatican in Rome, scented with incense and blazing with colour; painted monuments, frescoes and beams; embroidered vestments; gold and silver plate reflecting candlelight. This splendour was depleted by puritanical self-righteous vandalism in the sixteenth and seventeenth centuries, but here and there, notably in the great church of St Peter Mancroft, an idea of past magnificence survives.

Norfolk was the great county for church-building, almost a thousand being built between the eleventh and sixteenth centuries, far more than in any other county. Most of these were built upon the sites of earlier churches, recorded in Domesday Book and, of the total, more than 600 were still in use at the end of the twentieth century. They are an astonishing record of taste and technology, built at a period when almost all who worshipped in them lived in houses constructed of wattle and daub, or whatever local brick or stone (there was little in Norfolk) was to hand, so stone was imported, sometimes from Normandy, flints mined, bricks baked and beams carved.

The design and scale of the buildings depended upon the wealth of their patrons. They ranged from simple little churches (like the eleventh-century All Saints at Waterden, now alone in the fields) to the equally isolated, near-cathedral of St Peter and St Paul at Salle with its tower 111 ft high. Country churches might have round towers if built of flint and if no stone was available for masonry to support corners. In the fertile fenland, the great churches, such as those of Walpole St

Peter and Terrington St Thomas, reflected the wealth of their benefactors. Sometimes modesty and ostentation came together, as at Tittleshall, where the humble church of St Mary came to house the mausoleum and monuments of the Cokes, decorated with the sculpture of Roubilliac, Nollekens and Nicholas Stone.

After the Norman invasion the great religious houses of France set up satellite monasteries and nunneries; Norman bishops and abbots took their places beside Norman noblemen as rulers of the conquered country. Once the rule of Rome through Normandy had settled into place and been accepted, religion took hold of all aspects of life. Since Christianity laid such stress upon miracles, there was no reason why the miraculous should not be accepted not only as the answer to otherwise inexplicable mysteries, but as the inspiration and motive force of practical undertakings. Perhaps the most remarkable of these was the creation of a destination for pilgrims from all over the country, and, indeed, Europe, in the remote village of Walsingham.

Rural England was rife with miraculous tales, some of which caught the imagination of the devout, and this was the most potent. The wife of the lord of the manor of Walsingham, Richeldis de Fauvraches, dreamed that the Virgin Mary had commanded her to build a replica of the House of the Annunciation – the original was said to have been miraculously transported from Nazareth to Loreto in Italy – and the chosen site would be indicated by the appearance of a spring of water. This was duly found and enclosed within a simple shrine and a little wooden 'Holy House' was built. Then, in 1153, Richeldis's son began to build a priory there for Augustinian monks and this became a repository for miraculous relics. The most notable was a phial of the Virgin Mary's milk, drawn off from a flagon at a church in Paris; there was also a large fragment of bone, said to be St Peter's finger-joint; and, when Erasmus visited Walsingham, he wrote of the shrine, 'You will say it is the seat of the gods, so bright and shining it is all over with jewels, gold and silver', and there he was given a scented splinter of wood from a bench on which the Virgin was said to have sat. Meanwhile the 'holy spring' was said to have demonstrated remarkable curative powers.

Attracted by the growing importance of the site, the Franciscan Grey Friars arrived in the middle of the fourteenth century and built an enormous church beside the spring. Walsingham became an even more important place of pilgrimage than Canterbury, equivalent in the acquisition of virtue to visiting Nazareth itself. The beautiful Slipper Chapel was then built half a mile from the shrine for pilgrims to leave their shoes before completing the journey barefoot, while in the prospering village itself, some twenty inns opened to house and feed them. Every English monarch made the pilgrimage, including King Henry VIII, who was to bring about the downfall of this, amongst so many lesser shrines.

The dissolution of the monasteries – and, of course, the redistribution of their vast wealth by the King – brought about a change in the religious stance of the English people, and in their social structure, and decades of bloody religious persecution and war. The great church of Our Lady of Walsingham was demolished, leaving only the soaring arch of the east window flanked by two turrets and some archaeological remains in the grass. The statue of the Virgin was taken to London by Thomas Cromwell, the King's chief executive in destroying the monasteries, and burned in the garden of his house in Chelsea. The loss was deeply mourned by those brought up under the spiritual rule of Rome:

> Levell levell with the ground
> The towres doe lye
> Which with their golden, glittering tops
> Pearsed once to the sky . . .

> Oules do scrike where the sweetest himnes
> Lately were songe
> Toades and serpentes hold their dennes
> Where the palmers did thronge . . .

> Weepe, weepe O Walsingham
> Whose dayes are nightes,
> Blessings turned to blasphemies,
> Holy deeds to dispites.

> Sinne is where our Ladye sate,
> Heaven turned is to hell,
> Sathan sittes where our Lord did swaye,
> Walsingham oh farewell.

So, around the ruined shrine frogs spawned in the holy well and the village relapsed into obscurity, the deep countryside closing in, and sank into poverty. Occasionally visited by Georgian tourists, it was regarded as a picturesque ruin with a wishing well and a curative spring. As Thomas Wale, a Cambridgeshire merchant in the Baltic trade noted,

> Saw here the ruin of the old cloister . . . arches and large high walls, cold baths and Holy Wells; the one with a stone to kneel upon with the naked knee and, after crossing himself with ye water (which is all spring water and never freezes) and drinking a glass of ye water and wishing for any matter or thing . . . such shall be sure and happen. The other well is for dipping people for certain complaints.

Such visitors became increasingly rare and Walsingham became a forgotten village with a large Georgian house – ironically, a seat of a Quaker family, the Gurneys – on the site of the monastery and the gaunt ruin of the east end of the abbey a folly on its lawn.

So it remained until the First World War brought back an anguished longing for spiritual reassurance, and one manifestation of this was High Anglo-Catholicism. In 1931 the rector of Walsingham, the Revd Hope Patten, himself 'high church', set about trying to revive Walsingham as a centre of pilgrimage but did so against opposition both from within the Church of England and amongst Roman Catholics, who considered it to have been their pilgrimage. The Gurneys refused to allow the holy well – now considered a 'wishing well' in their garden – to be restored, Lady Gurney remarking that she did not want her lawn ruined by pilgrims. Happily a freehold building site became available just outside the Abbey walls and a blocked well discovered there. So it was announced that the holy spring had re-appeared and this became the site for a new shrine and a new destination for pilgrimage.

The revival of Walsingham has not been entirely happy.

There was rivalry between the different Christian doctrines and the Catholics acquired and restored the former Slipper Chapel, which had been used as a barn, as their centre of pilgrimage: at one time signposts, both indicating 'To the Shrine', pointed in opposite directions. The Russian Orthodox Church bought the redundant railway station on the edge of the village, filled the former ticket office with icons and decorated its roof with little golden, onion-shaped domes. Then, in 1961, the handsome fourteenth-century parish church of St Mary, was gutted by a mysterious fire.

Nevertheless, regular pilgrimages of both Anglicans and Catholics continue, and motorists navigating the narrow, leafy lanes around Walsingham may find themselves embedded in a slow procession of hymn-singing pilgrims; others may be shouldering crosses, walking barefoot and a few even walking backwards towards the ancient magnet that has drawn their predecessors for nearly a millennium.

This was the most famous shrine in Norfolk, but there were others. It was a time of saints and relics. Among the saints was St Edmund, the martyred Saxon king, who may have met his death tied to a tree and pierced with Danish arrows before being beheaded; an ancient tree felled near Diss within living memory was said to have iron arrowheads embedded in its heart. He was followed by others, ranging from the ridiculous to the sublime. At one extreme was St William in the Wood, a small boy, who, it was alleged, had been ritually crucified by Jews in woodland outside Norwich. He was canonised and his cult, fostered by those who saw their Jewish neighbours as rivals in commerce, fuelled mounting anti-Semitic hysteria which led to massacres in Norwich and Lynn and to years of persecution culminating in the expulsion of the survivors from England in 1290, not to return until Oliver Cromwell invited them back during the Commonwealth.

At the opposite, respectable, extreme came St Julian, who was, in fact, a woman. Born in 1343, she was a nun, who became an anchoress, or hermit, at the age of thirty and took the name of the church which provided her with a cell. Her meditations resulted in one of the first books to be written by a woman in English, *Revelations of Divine Love*, a tract that was the antithesis of the bigoted and blood-thirsty cult of St William in the Wood. Six centuries later she was the patron saint of the successful movement for the ordination of women.

There were several other, less-publicised Norfolk saints, amongst them St Walstan of Bawbergh, a hermit and confessor; St Margaret of Hoveton, who, like William, was said to have been murdered in a wood; and St Withburga of Dereham, an Anglo-Saxon princess, who founded a nunnery, which was destroyed by the Danes, and whose body was reputed to have been stolen by the monks of Ely in emulation of the Venetian capture of the body of St Mark from Alexandria. There were also a number of locally-canonised saints, amongst them,

> John Schorne, gentleman born,
> Conjured the devil into a boot

and apparently imprisoned him there; and Maid Ridibone, who was said to have fallen into a mill-wheel and been killed only to recover, with no bones broken; restored to life by the intercession of St Alban and then so revered that a chapel was dedicated to her in Cromer church.

In this credulous age there was a booming trade in holy relics credited with miraculous powers. Amongst these were said to be the head of St John the Baptist at Trimingham; a piece of the True Cross at Bromholm; 'The Smock of St Audrie' at Thetford, regarded as a cure for toothache; finally, 'The Great Sword of Winfarthing', before which a bored, or bullied, wife could light a candle every Sunday for a year in the expectation of shortening her husband's life.

In addition to such oddities there were many monastic institutions which, recovering from Danish plunder or founded thereafter, were the settings of many admirable lives dedicated to worship, learning and agriculture. More than fifty monastic houses were established in Norfolk: from the massive, such as the Benedictine foundations by the cathedral at Norwich and the Cluniac order's magnificent priory near the castle at Castle Acre to modest rural friaries that were virtually religious farmsteads. The principal orders which flourished after the coming of the Normans were the Benedictines (Binham and Wymondham as well as Norwich); the Cluniac order (Thetford and Bromholm as well as Castle Acre); the Augustinians (Walsingham, Thetford, North Creake and nearby Peterstone); Cistercians (Marham and Field Dalling and other remote villages); Carmelites (Burnham Norton); there were also foundations of other, less familiar orders, including the Knights Templar and Knights Hospitaller.

Most of these followed a pattern: the church and cloister; dormitory and refectory for the monks or nuns; often there would be a library as the seat of learning. Yet they fell into two separate categories: the monasteries with land and endowments, notably those of the Cluniac order, which became less popular as they grew richer, and the friaries, founded in reaction to them, which renounced worldly wealth and subsisted on charity. Small friaries were established by the Dominicans, Franciscans, Augustinians and Carmelites in the towns and their remains survive in Norwich, Great Yarmouth, King's Lynn, Thetford and Blakeney. All of these, like Walsingham, fell to King Henry's axe in the third decade of the sixteenth century.

Although the Reformation was widely welcomed in Norfolk for cutting down the power and wealth of overbearing clerics, there followed bewildering years of counter-Reformation and persecution. King Henry was succeeded by his daughter Mary, who married King Philip II of Spain and was, of course, a Catholic, reversing the dictates of the previous reign so that it was now the Protestants who were persecuted and burned at the stakes as heretics. After five years, she died and a Protestant, Queen Elizabeth, came to the throne and it was the Catholics' turn to be out of favour again. Yet religious persecution was nothing new for it had long been applied to those who tried to interpret Christianity in a fresh way, as it had to the Jews, who did not subscribe to it. Shortly before the Reformation, followers of one such movement, known as the Lollards, who sought a fresh interpretation of the Bible, and were led by John Wycliffe, who had first translated it into English, had suffered terribly, particularly under the persecution of the Bishop of Norwich, Henry Despenser (d. 1406). Numbers of the most active were burned alive with full ecclesiastial ceremony in the 'Lollards' Pit' beside the river near Bishop's Bridge. More suffered here during the reign of Queen Mary, ghastly processions, with chanting priests flanking the condemned heretics, passing the cathedral and crossing the medieval bridge to the stake beside the gently flowing water of the Wensum. Bishop's Bridge still spans the placid water and, where a memorial stone commemorates the martyrs of Lollards' Pit, picnic tables have been set on the smooth slopes of municipal lawn.

But sixteenth-century Norfolk did produce one remarkably moderate cleric, Matthew Parker (1504–75), who managed not only to defy the current religious establishments and survive, but became Archbishop of Canterbury. His courage was demonstrated by his opposing the judicial looting of Cambridge University (where he had been educated) by King Henry VIII, as well as by having been chaplain to his doomed queen, Anne Boleyn. In Norwich during Kett's rebellion, he preached to the rebels on Mousehold Heath, urging them to lay down their arms and go home, so he was lucky to escape more than threats. During the persecution of Queen Mary's reign, he had been a friend of the reforming priest, Thomas Bilney, who was burned in the Lollards' Pit, and he took up the cause of the 'pretender', Lady Jane Grey, although such connections necessitated him having to live 'in concealment' for a time.

On the accession of Queen Elizabeth I, he was appointed Archbishop of Canterbury and made efforts to unite the warring Christian factions within the Church of England. He reduced the forty-two principles of doctrine to the Thirty-Nine Articles, that became the basis of theological practice, producing the Prayer Book of 1549 and a new translation of the Bible. Hated by extremists inclined both to Roman Catholicism and to Puritanism, he helped lay the foundations of the future Church of England.

In religion, as in politics, there was a strong strain of

independence in Norfolk people, who always liked to 'do different', perhaps because of their long history of invasion and alien rule. Just as many had objected to the dominance of the Catholic monasteries, so some of the old families – notably in the west of the county – stubbornly kept to their former religion when the Church of England was founded. Perhaps Catholicism had been associated so long with Norman dominance in the distant past, and the riches of the religious institutions they founded seen as more material than spiritual, but the East Anglicans embraced the plainer, simpler form of religion that came with the division of England by the Civil War. Just as the Cavaliers tended to favour Catholicism and 'high church' practices, so the Roundheads promoted Puritanism. Some of those churches that had escaped the destruction of their finery – the smashing of statues, the burning of vestments and the whitewashing of frescoes – at the time of the Reformation, now suffered similar vandalism at the hands of the Puritans.

The Civil War had brought conflict and confusion to the Church of England in Norfolk, as throughout England; even a moderate, like the Bishop of Norwich, Joseph Hall (1574–1656), suffered from Puritan zeal although he had sympathised with them. Not only was he driven from the Bishop's Palace but the cathedral was desecrated. 'It is not other than tragical,' he wrote,

to relate the carriage of that furious sacrilege, whereof our eyes and ears were the sad witnesses . . . Lord, what work was here! What a clattering of glasses! what a beating down of walls! what tearing up of monuments! what pulling down of seats! what wresting out of irons and brass from the windows and graves! what defacing of arms! what demolishing of curious stone-work! what tooting and piping upon the destroyed organ-pipes! and what a hideous triumph on the market-day . . . when, in a kind of sacriligious and profane procession, all the organ-pipes, vestments, both copes and surplices, together with the leaden cross, which had been newly sawn down from over the Green-yard pulpit, and the service-books and singing-books that could be had, were carried to the fire in the public marketplace; a lewd wretch walking before the train, his cope trailing in the dirt, with a service-book in his hand, imitating in impious scorn the tune and usurping the words of the Litany used formerly in the Church.

The Restoration brought a new balance and toleration to religion but it was never settled in East Anglia and this was not an end to the divergence in religious taste. Just as the monasteries had been identified with the Norman landowners, so the Church of England with its handsome churches, their tombs for the rich and their pews for the squire became interwoven with the social structure. Those who defied it increasingly sought an alternative and this they found in a variety of dissenting off-shoots from the mainstream of English Christianity. This involved not only simpler, more direct forms of service but plain 'meeting houses' instead of the splendid churches with altars, rood screens, pulpits and carved angels gazing down from the rafters. The theological basis of this was that religious finery had been man-made and that Jesus Christ had been the son of a carpenter and had followed a modest way of life.

Several such groups, including the Congregationalists and the Baptists, had been formed by the end of the seventeenth century and had established themselves in two dozen Norfolk towns and villages, reinforcing home-grown Puritanism and religious ideas that had come across the North Sea; the most powerful of these were those of Martin Luther and Thomas Bilney, the Lollard, burnt at Norwich, who was to be called 'The Luther of East Anglia'. Yet, a century later, such dissent was not seen as any threat to the Church of England, although one Norfolk parson is recorded as calling the dissenters 'impertinent'.

Then blew the radical whirlwind of John Wesley (1703–91), the charismatic preacher, who made more than forty visits to Norfolk during his continuous travels around the country, during which he is said to have delivered 40,000 sermons. A well-educated man with some influential family connections, he had been in America and been influenced by evangelical movements there. The result was Methodism, the following of the 'method' of life laid down by the New Testament, so by-passing much of the dogma and ritual added to Christianity over the past eighteen centuries; indeed, Wesley eventually ordained his own bishops. This was seen as liberation by those working people who felt uncomfortable in the parish churches dominated by the higher strata of the social hierarchy. So, instead, many villagers crowded into meeting houses and chapels, singing hymns as lustily as popular songs without fear of a disapproving glance from the squire's lady.

After Wesley's death, Methodism continued to flourish but tended to fragment into smaller sects, such as the Primitive Methodists, whose little box-like chapels arose all over the county, ringing with loud proletarian hymns, in a direct challenge to the established church, one mid-Victorian parish clerk writing contemptuously of 'Ranters' Meetings'. By the end of the nineteenth century, the Wesleyan and Primitive Methodist chapels together covered the county almost as thickly as its parish churches.

One nonconformist group that made a huge impact despite its small numbers were the Quakers, or the Society of Friends, whose converts included the Gurney, Buxton, Barclay and Hoare families, who moved from the traditional Norfolk occupations into both banking and social reform.

Later, far less self-effacing nonconformists joined the Salvation Army, intent on making the maximum impact on the public with uniforms, bands and street-corner campaigns based upon 'citadels' rather than chapels. Founded in 1877, it was soon invading Norfolk and, in 1883, the vicar of East Dereham reported,

> The Salvation Army have sent a detachment into Dereham, who are carrying on an 'assault and bombardment against the Citadel of Sin'. Whether the citadel is the parish or only the theatre, which they have hired, I do not know . . . But I doubt the immense number of instantaneous conversions recorded in the *War Cry*, a copy of which I purchased for a halfpenny from an Hallelujah Lass.

With the arrival of the Hanoverian kings, the Church of England had at last had time to settle down to becoming the familiar background to English lives that it was to remain, with the Roman Catholic minority regarded as mildly eccentric rather than subversive. So the eighteenth century became the first of two golden ages of the parson – the Georgian and the Victorian – as a lynch-pin of rural life, and it was a

Norfolkman who set the pattern of the Rowlandsonian figure of popular imagination.

There already was a literary tradition amongst the Norfolk clergy, reaching far back but firmly established earlier in the century by two particular clerics, Humphrey Prideaux (1648–1724), Dean of Norwich, and Francis Blomefield (1705–52), rector of Fersfield. When the former was appointed, the cathedral was still strewn with the wreckage of the Puritans' sack and he restored the founder's tomb. Yet he was by education an orientalist and his contemporaries knew him as an author, notably of *The Life of Mahomet* and an immense work connecting the Old and New Testaments, books that ran through many editions but are now long forgotten.

The works of Blomefield are, however, still quoted as sources for he was the author of the massive, dry *History of Norfolk*, which ran to eleven volumes in one edition. As a boy in Thetford, he had begun collecting scraps of recorded, or remembered, history and his zealous research led him to send out questionnaires two centuries before that became commonplace. He had written two-thirds of his history when, having refused to be inoculated against smallpox on the ground that it was an affliction sent by God, he died of it and his work was completed by another rector, Charles Parkyn of Oxborough.

Their successor was quite different and his work, unlike theirs, is still in print. James Woodforde (1740–1803) is immortalised by his own diaries which recorded his daily life in the parish of Weston Longville near Norwich. Because of his style and, particularly, his relish in describing his enormous meals ('We had a very genteel Dinner, Soals and a Lobster Sauce, Spring Chicken boiled and a Tongue, a Piece of rost beef, Soup, a Fillet of Veal rosted with Morells and Trufles, and a pigeon Pye for the first Course – Sweetbreads, a green Goose and Peas, Apricot Pye, cheesecakes, stewed Mushrooms and Trifle'), he has long been ripe for parody. Yet he demonstrated the value of the educated parson (he had graduated from New College, Oxford) to village life in binding the social structure with the cement of his learning, preaching and good works; one of the reasons, perhaps, why England did not become a seed-bed for revolution, like France.

His five volumes of diaries also give a sharp-focused picture of familiar historical events as they were seen at the time. For example, on 29 November 1798, he noted,

> Great Rejoicings at Norwich today on Lord Nelson's late great and noble Victory over the French near Alexandria in Egypt. An Ox rosted whole in the Market-Place &c. This being a day of general Thanksgiving Mr. Cotman read Prayers this morning at Weston Church, proper on the Occasion. Dinner today, Leg of Mutton rosted &c. I gave my Servants this Evening after Supper some strong Beer and some Punch to drink Admiral Lord Nelson's Health on his late grand Victory . . .

The coming of aeronautics he reported on 1 June 1765:

> About 3 o'clock this Afternoon a violent Tempest arose at Norwich . . . very loud Thunder and strong white Lightening with heavy Rain . . . immediately after which Mr. Decker's Balloon with Decker himself in a boat attached to it ascended from Quantrell's Gardens and very majestically. It was out of sight in about 10 minutes . . . I saw it from Brecondale Hill and it almost went over my Head . . . A vast Concourse of people were assembled to see it. It was rather unfortunate that the weather proved so unfavourable – but added greatly to the Courage of Decker that he ascended so very soon after the Tempest.

Another Norfolk parson of that breed was Edmund Nelson (1722–1802), the father of the great admiral. He had graduated from Caius College, Cambridge, and remained a scholar by inclination. He was a modest man without ambition, confessing, 'As to the Society in Me, I never mixed with the World eno' at a proper period of Life to make it entertaining or valuable on any account, except to make my family comfortable when near me and not unmindfull of me when at a distance'.

When rector of Burnham Thorpe – he also had the livings of Burnham Ulph and Burnham Norton – he visited Bath to take the medicinal waters but otherwise was content with his lot, even in winter when he might have to walk through the snow from one church to another: 'I neither see, nor hear, nor know of any body or anything; darkness and light to me are alike; all is hush and High noon as at Midnight. No matter, I have seen eno' and am perfectly at ease about those matters.'

Widowed and left to care for a large family at the age of forty-five, he had to rely on village girls to look after his children in a house as cold as, and not much more comfortable than their own. His son Horatio was said to speak with a Norfolk accent and, indeed, the family spanned the social strata. How closely his life corresponded with that of village people was demonstrated when Horatio, returned home from the West Indies with his bride, Fanny. She had been accustomed to luxury, servants constantly on call, and warmth – if not of the Caribbean sun, then of a well-heated house in London, or Bath – and she hated it, her father-in-law joking, 'Mrs. N. takes large doses of the bed' when at the Parsonage. As soon as her husband returned to sea, she left for the fashionable comfort of Swaffham, taking lodgings, it is thought, at Montpelier House, the namesake of her home on the Caribbean island of Nevis.

Two friends of his demonstrated the range of character in the Norfolk clergy. His neighbour at North Creake was an equally bookish parson but one with social position and an income to match: the Revd Charles Poyntz, who became a canon of Windsor. He was the brother-in-law of Earl Spencer, who owned land in north-west Norfolk and in whose gift was the living, and could afford his passion for book-collecting and to build a library, Edmund Nelson writing, 'Dr. Poyntz . . . has made a handsome Room at Creake, detached from the House and intends the collection for the use of the publick under certain regulations'.

A very different cleric was the Revd Dixon Hoste (1751–1826) of Tittlesham, whose son William was taken to sea by Horatio Nelson. Dixon Hoste had the reputation of a sponger and was ambitious, hoping for a bishopric through the influence of his powerful landlord Thomas Coke of Holkham.

Finally, Coke himself tired of the old spendthrift when he failed to pay his rent for twelve years, evicting him from Godwick Hall, and, although promising that a new rectory would be built, gave him 'a small smoky house' at Litcham. 'I have felt and still feel his late neglect of me most poignantly,' Hoste complained to Coke's agent, unable to see himself through others' eyes. He was eventually to be buried in the same church as his landlord.

This time was remembered in the 1850s by an old parishioner of Dereham, who told his vicar that he remembered 'Old Mr. Thomas', his Georgian predecessor, 'catechizing the boys under the pulpit, and teaching them prayers at Christmas-time, and always giving them a pair of shoes and stockings . . . Vicar Thomas was the last of the Vicars who wore the three-cornered hat and cauliflower wig.'

The long somnolent afternoon of the Church of England lasted through most of the eighteenth and much of the nineteenth century, broken only by the rowdy hymn-singing of the dissenters in the chapel down the road from the church and, for much of this time, the Diocese of Norwich was known as the Dead See. Perhaps in reaction to the success of nonconformist Christianity, parish priests asserted themselves increasingly throughout Queen Victoria's reign. Clergymen of strong personality would dominate their parishes, but elsewhere it would be the squire, and he could impose a discipline upon congregations that drove them even more into the matey embrace of the chapels.

One such was Sir William Haggard, the squire of West Bradenham, whose ways with churchgoing were described by his son Rider:

> My father was regularly in attendance at church. We always sat in the chancel on oak benches originally designed for the choir. If he happened to be in time himself and other parishioners, such as the farmers' daughters, happened to be late, his habit was, when he saw them enter, to step into the middle of the nave, produce a very large old watch . . . and hold it aloft that the sinners as they walked up the church might become aware of the enormity of their offence.
>
> He always read the Lessons and read them very well. There were certain chapters, however, those which are full of names both in the Old and New Testaments, which are apt to cause difficulty. It was not that he was unable to pronounce those names, for having been a fair scholar in his youth he did this better than most. Yet when he had finished the list it would occur to him that they might have been rendered more satisfactorily. So he would go back to the beginning and read them all through again.
>
> At the conclusion of the service no one in the church ventured to stir until he had walked down it slowly and taken up his position on a certain spot in the porch. Here he stood and watched the congregation emerge, counting them like sheep.

The parishioners mostly seemed to accept all this in a religious and social haze. While many accepted Christian teaching, this was often overlaid by obscure dogma and biblical references, which began at Sunday School for children, so that the Old Testament tended to bear down upon them. One nineteenth-century Dereham baby bore the name of Mahershallalashbaz Tuck because, when his father decided to give him the shortest name in the Bible, which was Uz, the clergyman conducting the christening demurred. So he announced his characteristically Norfolk decision, 'Well, if he cannot have the shortest he shall have the longest.' Otherwise, attendance at church was seen as a social obligation, absence was noted by the social hierarchy and 'chapel folk' were regarded as the social rebels they sometimes were.

Ancient memories remained and, in the deep country, superstition. One particularly able and perceptive clergyman, Benjamin Armstrong (1817–90), who was vicar of East Dereham for thirty-eight years, wrote in his diary for 1864,

> A poor woman, whose child is about to be baptized will call her Withburga, after our local saint – a name probably never given in Dereham since the days of the saint herself. The 19th. century has not produced universal knowledge. I have been with two parishioners this week who are really and truly persuaded that they are bewitched, a notion that is very far from being extirpated yet in these country parts. I have known a woman walk miles to consult a 'wise woman' as to the cause of her husband's illness, and I have known another woman who told me that she thought her husband had been 'overlooked' – i.e. that someone had cast an evil eye upon him.

As a diarist and reflector of his age, Armstrong – a handsome, smiling man with little mutton-chop side-whiskers in his photograph of 1865 – was Woodforde's successor. In place of the latter's narrow horizons of village, church, heavy-laden dining-table and, in the distance, Norwich, he was heavily involved in church politics and social welfare, and he travelled widely at home and abroad by rail and steamer. He was a link between the Georgians and the Victorians, knowing men who had fought under Nelson's and Wellington's command, and children who would live to see travel in Space. He was himself every inch a Victorian paternalist, noting in his diary that he dined with a well-to-do friend named Hicks at Watton, where 'the dinner, though cold, was a luxurious one with plenty of claret and champagne. At eight the whole party went to a conversazione got up by Hicks in the Town Hall, the object being to show goodwill to the lower classes by mingling with them.'

He ruled his family with what he would have seen as wisdom and beneficent discipline. 'A young man wrote to me requesting to become a suitor to one of my daughters,' he noted. 'Although there is no objection to the young man personally yet the letter admitted of but one reply, seeing he is not of age, is not being trained for any profession, and his family, I fear, not well off. Wrote as kindly as I could. I think my daughter is not so hard hit but that she will soon get over it.'

He visited the Great Exhibition of 1851 and heard Charles Dickens read from *The Pickwick Papers*, noting 'not only did he remind me of a hairdresser but there is an unmistakeable look of ill-temper about him, contrasting very unfavourably with Thackeray's genial face'. He marvelled at the brilliance of electric light and mourned the passing of the age of sail: 'Nothing can be more hideous than the appearance of these iron vessels as compared with the majestic ships to which we have been accustomed'.

Not all Victorian clergy could match his strict standards. In 1852, he found the parish of Cawston 'shamefully neglected, the Rector, Mr. Bulwer, a cousin of the author Bulwer Lytton, employing his time in the elevating task of mending pots and kettles ... The curate ... was clad in check trousers, buff waistcoat and holland blouse, no neckerchief and a nautical cap. I never saw anyone so unlike a clergyman in all respects. Such a person must be quite ignorant of the dignity and solemnity attaching to his office.' But there was sometimes a gleam of humour in Armstrong's eye, as when he recorded a churchyard epitaph, 'Be thou what you think I ought to have been'.

Country clergymen – there were many of them, prompting the saying, 'Norfolk is full of parsons and oak trees' – seemed to fall into stereotypes over the centuries: the bucolic Georgian, ever-ready to ride to hounds or drain a bowl of punch, and the worthy Victorian, wreathed in clouds of theological theories and beset by those of Charles Darwin; then, with the twentieth century, the exponent of muscular Christianity. He performed as effectively in the parish as in the pulpit, so becoming a cohesive force in the society of his time. Two who come to mind are Jack Bowers and Aubrey Aitken.

Bowers (1854–1926) was appointed Rector of North Creake, Archdeacon of Lynn and Bishop of Thetford in 1903, and in 1914 dropped the first of these, moving from his rectory to The Close in Norwich. Part-Scottish, and the son of the chief engineer of the Royal Mail Line at Southampton, he was a communicator and preacher of genius, his deep, rumbling voice still well-remembered at the end of the century; his top-hatted gaitered figure said to have been the inspiration for 'Canon Fontwater', the 'Pocket Cartoon' character invented by Sir Osbert Lancaster, whose family he had known. He was a favourite of Norfolk railwaymen, who joined the congregation of three thousand at the funeral in 1926 of the jolly clergyman who was sometimes called 'the Bishop of the Great Eastern Railway'. Such was the power of his personality that half a century after his death, I, as his grandson, still basked in the afterglow.

His son and another grandson became great players on the rugby field, as did a young man he confirmed, Aubrey Aitken (1912–88). He, too, became a popular suffragan bishop in Norfolk – the Bishop of Lynn – and president of the Norwich Rugby Club as well as vice-president of Norwich City Football Club. A tall, well-built, handsome man, square of jaw and bright of eye, Aitken preached with splendid theatricality and conviction; even after he lost his voice to a cancer operation he continued to address his audience in a metallic, artificial voice through a loudspeaker. In his obituary, the *Eastern Daily Press* declared, 'He embodied . . . a direct faith, breadth of sympathy, companionable instincts and a deep attachment to his native land and its people. Here was a good man who believed that it was better to light a candle than curse the darkness.' Appropriately, it was Bishop Aitken who dedicated a memorial to Bishop Bowers in North Creake church, and their memorials now face each other in the choir of Norwich Cathedral.

Both men belonged to the time when a priest could be found in almost every parish and was usually a graduate of Oxford or Cambridge; moreover, in the larger parishes he would be assisted by a curate. There was plenty of work apart from taking the regular services in church: visiting parishioners, taking responsibility for the Sunday School, organising fund-raising activities like amateur entertainments and the parish fête, which was usually held in the rectory garden. Then there were activities with worthy oganisations such as the Boy Scouts, Girl Guides and Church Lads' Brigade.

As a man of education (oak bookcases of religious works were standard furnishing in parsons' studies), he would be expected to give a cultural lead in the parish. In many, those incumbents without private means lived frugal lives, bringing up families in large and chilly rectories with extensive gardens to maintain, if only to set an example in rural responsibility. Here and there a parish in the gift of a landowner would be considered 'a good living' and one such was North Creake, which owed its reputation to the largesse of Earl Spencer. Here, my grandfather occupied an enormous Victorian Gothic rectory, a large garden with surrounding woodland and 200 acres of glebe farmland. This enabled him to keep not only the usual domestic staff but a butler and a coachman.

Even in the heyday of country parsons that Rowlandson loved to caricature, the stately Georgian rectory at Stiffkey can have seen nobody to match the Revd Harold Davidson (1876–1937), the incumbent for more than a quarter of a century. His speciality was 'saving fallen women' but there were few in north-west Norfok, so, for this purpose, he made regular expeditions to Paris, then, after the First World War, to London. He sought not only prostitutes but those, like teashop waitresses, who might possibly consider prostitution as a career, sometimes bringing his catches back to Norfolk with him. Eventually he was accused of immoral practices with more than a thousand girls and in the Thirties became the nation's favourite source of scandal. Eventually he was tried before a church court at Westminster and ceremonially unfrocked in Norwich Cathedral. Unabashed, he proclaimed his own martyrdom, first fasting in a cage as a sideshow in a Blackpool amusement park, then displaying himself in a barrel and finally, in 1937, in a wonderful Old Testament climax, he preached at Skegness from within the cage of a lion, which promptly killed him. He lies buried at Stiffkey.

The decline in this nationwide network of well-manned parishes began just before the Second World War when some of the smaller and less populated were amalgamated with larger neighbours. In the 1950s and 1960s the process accelerated: most of the great, high-ceilinged vicarages and rectories were sold (most for less than £1,000) and amalgamations involved up to a dozen parishes. By the end of the century, the long-vacated houses of the clergy were selling for upwards of a quarter of a million pounds, usually as second homes for the urban rich and 'The Old Rectory' became a smart address for those concerned about social standing.

As for the clergy themselves, they usually lived in small, modern houses without architectural distinction and were strained not only by shuttling between their churches to take services, but by trying, when they did so, to maintain something of the old community spirit in all of them. Congregations had mostly shrunk since it was no longer the convention to be seen in church on Sunday and the middle-class newcomers, occupying their second homes, tended to be agnostic, or too exhausted by a week in a metropolitan office. That allowed, remarkable exceptions survived, dependent upon the character of the parson.

Some were true to the best of their predecessors; as robust and honourable as they were dutiful and devout. Such men were a potent force for good, remembered with affection long after their retirement. But there were also those who refused to retire despite obvious inadequacy; those who foisted their own taste in fashionable causes, or popular music, upon their parishioners, and those who did not bother to tend their flocks in the traditional manner. Yet, here and there, a church and parish would flourish, showing that the church and parson could still be a pillar of rural life.

V

Ideas

Sir Noël Coward's familiar quip about the flatness of Norfolk
blends with a general misconception that it is a dull, uninspiring county of worthies and yokels. But Norfolk was also the
source of ideas. Religious ideas were originally imported, of
course, but secular ideas were home-grown and seem to have
been germinated by historical conditions: the waves of
invasion and the consequent need for self-reliance in order to
survive and, as counter-balance, the long history of stern
paternalism from the early tribal chieftains, Roman
governors, regional kings, Norman overlords and the long
succession of feudal landowners that then took root. This
brought about the twin strains of independence of attitude and
also a mutual sense of responsibility between those content
with their lot as employer or employed.

The ideas that spread from Norfolk cannot, of course, all be
put in the category of religious, or political. It could be said
that, as an example of the eclectic nature of the county's
creativity, one of the originators of both hotels and advertising
was a Norfolkman named John Peck. It was he, a Norwich
merchant, who, in 1665, built an enormous coaching inn
capable of handling the passengers, coachmen and horses of
forty coaches a day at the intersection of roads linking
Norwich with Ipswich and London, at Scole. Then called the
White Hart – it is now the Scole Inn and one of the few inns in
England listed as being of Grade One in architectural
importance – Peck advertised it with a wildly elaborate, carved
sign that stretched across the road, decorated with allegorical
figures, hounds and a white hart. This cost the then huge sum
of more than £1,000 and was described by the Norwich sage,
Dr Thomas Browne, as 'the Noblest Signepost in England'. As

one of the first hotels in England, it could accommodate travellers in a dozen bedrooms and thirty of them in one enormous circular bed.

The seed-beds of ideas were, of course, the schools tended by the educationalists, who prepared other generators of ideas. Thomas Gresham (1519–79) of Holt was essentially a merchant, living in Antwerp and spreading British mercantile influence on the Continent with pan-European ideas that were not to be fulfilled for more than four centuries. As a leading financier of his day, he built the Royal Exchange in London at his own expense. This might have been enough for any Tudor grandee, but he also established a school in his own house at Holt, giving the management of it to the Fishmongers' Company. It flourishes today as the co-educational public school, Gresham's.

A very different course was followed by Matthew Vassar (1792–1868), who was born in East Tuddenham and was taken to America by his family at the age of four. Vassar became a successful brewer and the proprietor of an oyster saloon. Then, on a visit to London, he was impressed by the achievement of his friend, Thomas Guy, in founding a hospital and determined to emulate his good works. This was to be a women's college to match Yale and Harvard in academic quality and, in 1865, Vassar College was established at Poughkeepsie in New York State and lived up to his high expectations, although eventually becoming co-educational.

A century later, Nugent Monck (1878–1958) – Celtic Puritan, as he described himself – could also have been considered an educationalist in that he gave new confidence and originality to amateur theatricals. The professional theatre had long been established in Norfolk towns, and amateurs had performed in the country houses where they were guests and in which there were sometimes private theatres. Monck had arrived in Norwich before the First World War to produce a pageant and had settled there, starting his own company of amateurs. Then, in 1921, he took over the former Salvation Army 'citadel' which he converted into the Maddermarket Theatre. From that moment until he

retired in 1952, he produced all Shakespeare's plays and most of
the classics of the English theatre. His strength was self-
confidence, insisting on anonymity for his actors and saying,
'Anyone who wants to act for me must bring unquestioning
obedience and their own greasepaint'. Refusing most invitations
to tour with his company, he insisted that anyone who wished to
see his productions should come to the Maddermarket; they did.

Monck's panache gave a new standing to the amateur stage.
At the beginning of the century, my mother had written from
the Rectory at North Creake to a friend about her cousin, Sybil
Thorndike, even then a successful young actress, 'Sybil can't
come for Xmas. I'm rather relieved. I think I should be
dreadfully shy of acting before her.' After the success of the
Maddermarket, it is likely that she would have been happy to
hear the criticism of a professional.

Not surprisingly there have been far fewer inventors and
orginators of mechanical ideas in Norfolk than in industrial
counties, but one of them, George Manby (1765–1854), was
prolific and an ironical twist of fate turned his idea for killing
one man into another for saving the lives of countless others.
He was born at Denver in West Norfolk and educated at
Downham Market, where he claimed to have been a school-
friend of Horatio Nelson (thereby causing puzzlement to
generations of the admiral's biographers since he was seven
years Nelson's junior and there is no record of Nelson having
been at school there; he presumably confused him with a
namesake). Joining the Cambridgeshire militia (and reaching
the rank of captain), his original turn of mind came up with a
scheme for the assassination of Napoleon and, at the height of
fears of French invasion in 1803, he went to London to present
it to the Secretary for War. The idea was rejected but he was
sent to Great Yarmouth as barrack-master and it was while
there that he saw a ship wrecked on the sands in a storm,
resulting in the loss of some two hundred lives. This led to his
most celebrated invention and a plaque fixed to his house at
Gorleston in 1848 explains,

> In commemoration of the 12th February, 1808, on which day directly
> eastwards of this site the first life was saved from shipwreck by means of a

rope attached to a shot fired from a mortar over a stranded vessel, a method now universally adopted and to which at least 1,000 sailors of various nations owe their lives.

This was later developed into the lifeline fired by rocket.

He also designed a new type of lifeboat, harpoons, a dredger, a howitzer and, after watching a fire in Edinburgh, a chemical fire-extinguisher. Captain Manby was elected to the Royal Society in 1831, but otherwise not honoured, while his brother, Thomas, a naval officer, who was directly or indirectly responsible for many deaths at sea from gunshot or yellow fever, became an admiral.

Perhaps religious nonconformity was a spur to original thinking as it often appears in the background of the lives of Norfolkmen and women of ideas. One such was Sir James Smith (1759–1828), the botanist and founder of the Linnean Society. Born into a Unitarian family in Norwich at a time when a third of its population were nonconformist, it is also probable that he was influenced by the gardens that abounded within the city walls. More indirectly, his interest was fostered by four amateur botanists in the county: James Crowe, a surgeon of Lakenham and an authority on fungi, mosses and willows; another surgeon, John Pitchford, who was making a study of Carolus Linnaeus, the Swedish botanist, famous for re-classifying and naming plants according to species; the Revd Henry Bryant of Colby, who studied seaweeds, fungi and the diseases of wheat; and the apothecary Hugh Rose, who corresponded with William Hudson, the keeper of the Physic Garden in Chelsea. Then he left Norfolk for Edinburgh University to study medicine.

When Smith moved to London in 1782 to continue his studies at the celebrated Dr John Hunter's school of anatomy, he met Sir Joseph Banks, the President of the Royal Society. While breakfasting at Banks's house he heard that the botanical collections of Linnaeus, who had died four years before, were for sale and had been offered to his host for a price of £1,000. Banks had refused the offer but advised Smith to raise the money and buy it himself and this he managed to do. From the moment he acquired the collection and took premises in Chelsea to house it, his own career prospered: he was elected a member of the Royal Society and then himself founded the Linnean Society for the study of natural history.

Concentrating on botany rather than clinical medicine, Smith's reputation as a writer on botany rose to the point that, in 1797, he could afford to return to Norwich and spend only three months of the year in London. His written works included *English Botany* in thirty-six volumes and, later, *Introduction to Botany* and *English Flora*, but his greatest contribution to botany was in the re-classification of plants, replacing the old haphazard Latin nomenclature with the practical mixture of Latin and English that is still in use. He was knighted for this work in 1814 and, after his death in 1828, an obituarist wrote,

> He found the science of botany, when he approached it, locked up in a dead language; he set it free by transfusing it into his own. He found it a severe study, fitted only for the recluse; he left it of easy acquisition to all. In the hands of his predecessors, with the exception of his immortal master, it was dry, technical and scholastic; in his, it was adorned with grace and elegance and might attract the poet as well as the philosopher.

As a curious but fitting by-product of his life's work, Smith also wrote hymns which were sung by the Unitarian congregations of Norwich.

It was appropriate therefore that one of the leading botanists of the next generation, Sir William Hooker (1785–1865) was one of his protégés from Norwich. Hooker's discovery, while a boy, of a rare moss in woods near the city and his showing it to the recently-returned Smith prompted the latter to suggest he take up botany as a lifelong study. This was the great age of plant-hunting and for two decades Hooker travelled widely for this purpose, returning to become Professor of Botany at Glasgow University. Under the patronage of the Duke of Bedford, his name was put forward as a potential director of a new botanical research institution and, when this was opened at the Royal Gardens at Kew, he was duly appointed. Thus a vast range of botanical development and exploitation – ranging from the introduction of rubber to Malaya to the appearance of the fuchsia in English gardens – can be traced back through Hooker to Norwich and to James Smith.

The manipulation of money through banking was not, of course, an idea original to Norfolk but it did take on an unusual aspect in the county when it was allied to the Quakers. Elsewhere, it had often been a speciality of the Jewish community, which, forbidden to own land, found that it could create wealth by lending and managing money, and they had something in common with the Quakers of Norfolk in that they were a prosperous minority. But, unlike the Jews, the Quakers were not regarded as clever strangers; they were indigenous and they were trusted as familiar neighbours. So that when a prosperous weaving family like the Gurneys had surplus capital, they might lend or invest it, and from that it was a short step to banking. The Gurneys had long been 'lending, receiving, drawing drafts in London and, as merchants, carrying on all banking transactions' – as the historian of the family put it – before they began formal banking in the eighteenth century.

Then, in 1775, John and Henry Gurney founded the Norwich and Norfolk Bank. The *Norwich Mercury* reported in February of that year, 'We have heard that a new Banking House is proposed to be shortly established in this city on a new plan, where good bills on any part of Great Britain, or Ireland will be exchanged for drafts in London, and discounted for cash on reasonable terms, and bills abroad negotiated at the most favourable exchange; and business of any kind conducted with secrecy, safety and despatch'. The Gurneys intermarried with other families, notably the Buxtons, Barclays and Hoares and, finally, banking replaced weaving and sheep-farming as the foundation of their fortunes. The names of Barclay's and Hoare's banks remain at the summit of the financial world.

The money that flowed through the banks linked agriculture, industry and the expression of power and will, politics. The county did not throw up many significant politicians but those that it did include two of the country's greatest and most influential political figures.

Sir Robert Walpole (1676–1745), who has already been noted as a great landowner, was the most important but, to twentieth-century eyes, the least discernible as an historical character. He could be seen as a robust Norfolk squire – a full-faced man with heavy-lidded, worldly eyes – who lived much of his life in a house overlooking the Green Park in London rather than the rolling parkland around his Palladian mansion at Houghton; or seen as a manipulative politician, who sat in the House of Commons for most of four decades but gathered a magnificent collection of paintings. Holding office under Queen Anne and the first two King Georges, he had administered the Army, the Navy and the Treasury and it was as such that he became, in all but title, Prime Minister for twenty-one years.

As the historian A.J.P. Taylor has written,

> He was just as much the first modern Prime Minister we should recognise as Adam was the first man. He tied together Crown and Commons as no minister had done before. He sounded like a modern Prime Minister even though the sources of his power were different ... He took the venom out of politics and ended the era when men ruined or killed each other for political reasons ... Despite his lack of a party machine, he was the greatest of Parliamentary managers ... (although) he used means of influence which would now be regarded as corrupt. However, such means were the common fashion of his time and it is thanks to Walpole that British politics are still comparatively civilised.

More interested in domestic than in foreign affairs, he steered the Whig administration through a series of crises, beginning, a year after becoming 'first minister' and Chancellor of the Exchequer, with that of the South Sea Bubble. This was the boom in the shares of the South Sea Company, which traded particularly in slaves, and from which Walpole himself made money. When it became over-inflated and the bubble burst, Government stock fell but Walpole's steady hand on the helm saved it from collapse.

Unlike the more famous of his successors, Walpole's reputation did not rest upon one great crisis or confrontation, but rather on the deft negotiation of a succession of political shoals and rapids. Yet the image of the tough and cynical politician was only part of him. When he retired from politics to Houghton in 1742 as the newly-created Earl of Orford, to enjoy his park and his pictures, he wrote to a friend in London,

> This place affords no news, no subject of amusement to you fine gentlemen. Men of wit and pleasure about town understand not the language, nor taste the charms of the inanimate world; my flatterers here are all mutes, the Oaks and Beeches and the Chestnuts seem to contend, which shall best please the Lord of the Manor: they cannot deceive, they will not lie . . . Within doors we come a little nearer to real life and admire upon the almost speaking Canvas, all the airs and graces which the proudest of town ladies can boast. With these I am satisfied as they gratify me with all I wish and all I want and expect nothing in return which I am not able to give.

Sadly, Walpole had no heir to maintain the glories of Houghton as he would have wished, and most of his pictures were sold by his grandson to Catherine the Great and have remained in St Petersburg ever since. The house passed by descent through his daughter's marriage to the Earl [later Marquesses] of Cholmondeley but remains Sir Robert's monument. But his memorial is also the system of government by Prime Minister and Cabinet, which he introduced. After the Battle of Waterloo there had been talk of presenting Houghton to the Duke of Wellington, as the Duke of Marlborough had been rewarded with Blenheim; but the idea was dropped and the great house remained Walpole's.

He was the greatest of the Whig politicians to come out of Norfolk – Thomas Coke was to be another, but he never held Government office, and his most memorable influence was, as has been seen, in husbandry on the grand scale – yet the county's independence of mind did produce a politician who was to be even more famous on the world stage: Tom Paine.

Of all Norfolk men and women of ideas, the most influential must have been Tom Paine of Thetford (1737–1809). At a time when innovators usually relied upon social position and influential friends to make their case, let alone further it, this son of a Quaker stay-maker – surely the most unlikely parent for a political firebrand – was regarded by the rulers of his own country as a dangerous subversive but revered as a prophet in France and the future United States of America. Had he been no more than a hedgerow radical – and there were many such in the late eighteenth century – he would have been forgotten and less-regarded in his own time. His success was founded upon his brilliance as a phrasemaker.

The inventor of titles like *The Rights of Man*, *Common Sense* and *The Age of Reason*, could also write such trumpet-calls as 'These are the times that try men's souls'; 'The sublime and the ridiculous are often so nearly related that it is difficult to class them separately'; 'He pities the plumage, but forgets the dying bird'; 'My country is the world and my religion is to do good'. Nearly two centuries after his death, these still command the heights of radical rhetoric.

The roots of Tom Paine's political passion were in his father's Quakerism but ran deeper into the subsoil of the Norfolk tradition of independent thought and, perhaps, into memories of Kett's rebellion. Sermons in the Quaker meeting house in Thetford gave him a grounding in pacificism and the belief that humanitarianism could be an end in itself. Apprenticed to his father, he, too, became a corset-maker, later moving to Sandwich to open a shop selling 'ladies' foundation garments', and there he married the daughter of an exciseman and took up the more manly occupation of the customs service. Soon widowed, Paine, a sharp-featured, restless young man, moved to Lewes, where he joined the underground world of radical politics, becoming a member of the splendidly-named Headstrong Club to argue about the rightings of social wrongs.

It was then that he met Benjamin Franklin, the American political journalist and scientist, who gave him a letter of introduction, describing him as an 'ingenious, worthy young man', and this became, in effect, his passport to America, for which he sailed in 1774. He, too, became an energetic and influential political journalist, publishing, in 1776, a pamphlet called *Common Sense*, advocating complete independence from the British Crown. In 1787, he returned to England, and three years later his book *The Rights of Man* pouring scorn on the British constitution ('To inherit a Government is to inherit the People, as if they were flocks and herds'), was published. This book, which has been described by E.P. Thompson, the radical historian, as 'the foundation-text of the English working-class movement', was regarded as seditious in the atmosphere of fear that gripped Britain as the French Revolution lurched from radical reform to bloody class warfare. Paine articulated what many thought; not only the labourers but the artisans and many of the educated middle class, including Nelson.

In 1792, despite the dread of subversion and insurrection amongst the ruling classes, the unemployed Captain Nelson wrote – as has been noted – to his friend the Duke of Clarence to tell him, with supporting detail, about the plight of the Norfolk farmworkers. This was a bold move at such a time but it was in character. On his return from the West Indies with his wife, he had given up his first days of home leave to defend one of his men who had been charged with murder; later he was to appear in court to praise the former good character of the revolutionary Colonel Despard, who had attempted to kill the King and usurp the Government. Paradoxically, he was both a romantic patriot and a champion of the under-privileged, his sympathy with them deriving in part, perhaps, from his first-hand knowledge of poverty in Burnham Thorpe.

Nelson and Paine would have agreed on much. But their attitude to the institution of the monarchy and to the constitution could not have differed more. Nelson, despite his knowledge of the King's antipathy to himself, insisted that this was due to his political advisers and wrote to the Duke, 'Neither at sea, nor on shore, through the caprice of a Minister, can my attachment to my King be shaken'. Paine, however, had written of the monarchy, the monarch and the court: 'A banditti of ruffians overrun a country . . . and . . . the chief of the band contrived to lose the name of Robber in that of Monarch; and hence the origin of Monarchy and Kings'; and again,

Placemen, Pensioners, Lords of the Bedchamber, Lords of the Kitchen, Lords of the Necessary-house, and the lord knows what besides, can find as many reasons for monarchy as their salaries, paid at the expense of the country, amount to: but ask the farmer, the manufacturer, the merchant, the tradesman . . . the common labourer, what service the monarchy is to him, he can give me no answer. If I ask him what monarchy is, he believes it is something like a sinecure.

Since the monarchy was seen by most of the middle class as the foundation of national stability, Paine lost the sympathy of the rapidly growing English bourgeoisie, who saw him as a dangerous subversive and imagined the guillotine set up outside St James's Palace, a nightmare that was given ghastly realism in a caricature by Gillray. Throughout the 1790s, the county was racked by fears of subversion and even insurrection and these were expressed by its own political caricaturist, James Sayers (1748–1823), who had been born in Yarmouth and trained as a lawyer. Perhaps because his draughtsmanship could not compare with Gillray's, his caricatures were soon forgotten but they made an impact at the time. One showed Norfolk radicals seated on a bull, which was kneeling before animal-headed French revolutionaries, while Norwich Cathedral and 'Kett's castle' could be seen in the background; beneath, the caption ran,

> Since the days of old Kett, the republican Tanner,
> Faction always has seen us lost under her Banner,
> From our Country's best interests we've ever dissented,
> In War we're disloyal, in Peace discontented . . .
> In our City good patriots and levellers swarm,
> And our Sectaries bellow aloud for reform;
> Though from various Causes our Trade is decay'd,
> On this War all the blame we have artfully laid . . .
> Our John Bull we've cajoled to go down on his Knees
> To ask you for Peace and receive your Decrees.

Paine was charged with treason but managed to flee to France, where he was at first welcomed as a hero of social revolution. He was elected to the National Convention but was distrusted by Robespierre and imprisoned. While himself under the shadow of the guillotine during the Reign of Terror in 1794, he worked on *The Age of Reason*; he was released when, a year after his arrest, Robespierre himself was overthrown and executed.

The rise from corset-maker to hero of revolution in two

great foreign nations, and hero or villain in his own, was an extraordinary achievement. Paine was more than an agitator, for although he formed few practical plans for social reform, he presented theories which would be recognised by any twentieth-century socialist. But he did call for the cutting of government costs and defence expenditure and the introduction of income tax, which would rise to one hundred per cent at an annual income of £23,000. The money raised would fund education for all children, marriage, maternity and family allowances, financial and housing aid for the unemployed and old age pensions. 'The poor, as well as the rich, will then be interested in the support of Government,' he concluded, 'and the cause and apprehension of riots and tumults will cease. Ye who sit at ease and solace yourselves in plenty . . . have ye thought of these things?'

It was to end sadly. Returning to what was now the United States of America in 1802, he found his contribution to the birth of the nation largely forgotten. Five years later, living in New York, he died in poverty. In 1819, William Cobbett brought his remains home to England but their whereabouts are no longer known. His memorial is a statue in Thetford and the continuing passion and imagery of his radical rhetoric, which is still quoted after two centuries. Tom Paine stands beside Nelson and Coke as a great Norfolkman.

If Paine was what would one day be called a role model for future politicians of the Labour Party, the prototypes of future maternalists and paternalists were Elizabeth Fry (1780–1845) and Jeremiah Colman (1830–98), whose aggressive humanitarianism arose from the world of wealth and privilege that Paine denounced.

Betsy Gurney – as Elizabeth Fry was first known – was born into the Quaker family, which had become rich in the cloth trade and in banking, first living at Bramerton (with a town house in Norwich) and, in 1786, moving to Earlham Hall just outside the city. Betsy was a tall, serious, introspective, imaginative girl, who made self-absorbed notes in her diary such as: 'I am 17 today. Am I a happier creature than I was this

time twelve-months? I know I am happier: I think I am better. I
hope I shall be much better this day year . . . I hope to be quite
an altered person, to have more knowledge, to have my mind
in greater order and my heart, too . . . it is in such a fly-away
state.' She was excited and flustered by the opposite sex and
worried about her lack of religious conviction.

Then, two years after the family's arrival at Earlham, an
American Quaker, William Savery, visited Norwich to preach.
He was aged 48 and, perhaps, was something like Billy
Graham, the American evangelist of the mid-twentieth
century, for Betsy was entranced by him. She had attended his
meeting despite 'a very bad pain in my stomach' and sat in the
gallery, wearing new purple and scarlet boots. Savery was
introduced as a man who had preached to the savage Red
Indians of North America and had been in the country of the
enemy, the French, addressing them in their own language.
When he spoke he began by urging pacifism; this at a time
when fear of French invasion was extreme and a few months
after the churches of Norwich had held services of thanksgiving for the naval victory at the Battle of Cape St Vincent. He
continued to tell his provincial and inevitably narrow-visioned
congregation of the goodness and piety to be found in the Red
Indians and other 'heathens' amongst whom he had travelled.
This was exciting for an impressionable girl and soon Betsy
was seen to be 'a good deal agitated' and she began to weep.

That was the beginning. Soon after, she accepted an
invitation to stay in London and enjoy some fashionable
pleasures, but really it was in the hope of seeing Savery again.
Metropolitan life excited her and she made the most of herself,
noting, 'I did look quite pretty for me', and 'I do love grand
company', and was thrilled by a glimpse of the Prince of Wales,
gross as he was. But none of this would compare with the
impact of Savery, with whom she seems to have been
infatuated, while seeing her emotion as religious fervour.
When she heard him preach again, she confessed, 'I really did
cry with a sort of ecstasy' and that 'I first loved him for his
religion but the feelings of human nature are very apt to join
with the superior feelings of the heart'. But he was a married

man, twice her age, and she knew there could be no future for any imagined relationship. Then she had a curious dream: 'I dreamt that William Savery came and he was turned into a woman and that I did not love him as I do now, a good hint to myself.' She took the hint and charted her own way forward: 'I shall always love religion through him but must always love it away from him'. So her emotions began to be diverted into religion, eventually with militancy.

In 1800, Betsy married 'beneath her' another Quaker, Joe Fry, of a prosperous family which imported tea, coffee and cocoa, and they moved to London where they lived over the family firm's office in the City. She soon found that her husband did not measure up to the Gurneys' standards of industry, noting, 'Soon after waking, I hurt my dear Joseph by begging him to get up on account of business. He did not like my interfering ... and spoke rather sharply to me ... I mentioned I thought him not active in business.' But she became fond of him, was a dutiful wife and had borne him eight children by 1812 when his lack of business sense had reduced him almost to bankruptcy.

The Frys were saved from ruin by the Gurneys, who, together with their relations in the Hoare, Buxton and Barclay families, were now powerful in banking. Betsy had been trying to occupy herself with good works among the poor and had adopted the plain flowing Quaker dress, which suited her height and her manner for, as one of her daughters put it, 'My mother had three great gifts: stately presence, exquisite voice and unruffled sweetness of expression'.

Early in the following year, a fellow-Quaker took her on one of her visits to Newgate Prison in London, a place of Hogarthian horror. Shocked but fascinated, Betsy became aware of the contrast between herself and the ragged, half-starved women prisoners, mostly prostitutes and petty thieves. There was something of the actress in her and here a literally captive audience was clearly awe-struck by her. This was a stage for far more dramatic activity than that invited by the destitute and the drunkards of the streets of London outside the prison walls. She began regular visits and was particularly affected by the prisoners' children, who were without any kind of education and were growing up like wild animals. It struck her that she could start a little school for religious teaching as a counter to this institutionalised depravity.

Her school was a success, but Newgate presented infinite scope for good works in its depths of misery, for this was the age when hanging, or transportation to Australia, were usual punishments for crimes that might, two centuries later, be punished by a spell of 'service to the community', or regular visits to a probation officer. Early in 1817, Betsy wrote in her journal,

> My mind has been deeply affected in attending a poor woman, who was executed this morning. I visited her twice; this event has brought me into much feeling by some distressingly nervous sensations in the night . . . this witnessing the effect of the consequences of sin. The poor creature murdered her baby; and how inexpressible awful now to have her life taken away.

She visited other women in the condemned cells and pleaded for their reprieve. In one case she was successful but then came that of Harriet Skelton, the mother of eight children, who had been condemned for passing forged bank-notes. Her husband had already been hanged for the same crime when Elizabeth Fry took up her case with Lord Sidmouth, the Home Secretary. In her zeal, she went too far, enlisting the support of the Duke of Gloucester, with whom she had danced at a ball in Norwich in their youth, and, in an interview with Sidmouth, she admitted, 'in the efforts made to save her life, I too incautiously spoke of some in power'. Harriet Skelton was hanged.

Her ministering to prisoners went beyond Bible-reading and she discussed with them rules of behaviour and work they would like to undertake. The Newgate authorities, who had never thought beyond incarceration, realised that this might produce a more orderly prison and agreed. Within a few weeks of implementation, the new order she had proposed prompted her to record, 'Already, from being like wild beasts, the prisoners appear harmless and kind'. This began a series of fundamental reforms that spread throughout the prisons of Britain.

There were setbacks – one being another financial crisis for her husband in 1828 – but she had won fame and 'prison reform' became established as a good cause. She was granted an audience with Queen Victoria in 1840 and took the opportunity to preach at the sovereign. Although warned that she should only reply to questions from the Queen and be brief, Elizabeth told the Queen that, as she put it in her journal, her words 'reminded me of the words of Scripture "with the merciful I will show myself merciful" ', and she launched into her sermon. 'After a little more,' she recalled, 'she made a sort of sign for us to withdraw, when I stopped and said that I hoped the Queen would allow me to say that it was our prayer that the blessing of God might rest upon the Queen and her Consort.' Not content with this, she wrote asking for another audience to give her an opportunity for 'really speaking my mind as to the example she should set'. It was not granted.

But her message had spread across Europe and, as age changed the zealous reformer into a famous figure from the past, her place as a great civilising force was secure. She died of a stroke in 1845 and was buried at Barking in the Quaker cemetery.

In that same year, another philanthropist, Elizabeth Fry's brother-in-law, Sir Thomas Buxton (1786–1845), died in Norfolk. He had also been inspired by visits to Newgate and this had led him to write his *Inquiry into Prison Discipline*. Then their paths had diverged; his into the movement against slavery. He joined forces with William Wilberforce and, in 1822, succeeded him in leading the Parliamentary campaign which abolished slavery in British colonies and finally brought about the Abolition Act of 1833.

Elizabeth Fry was the most famous of a breed of educated, nonconformist Norfolk women, who took up the cause of social reform. One was a slightly older Norwich woman, Amelia Opie (1769–1853), the daughter of a radical and Unitarian doctor, James Alderson, who married the painter John Opie. A lively-minded girl with a strong, sensitive face, she had made a success as a novelist when she was converted to Quakerism. Becoming absorbed in the anti-slavery campaign and the improvement of workhouses, hospitals and prisons, she would attend the Norwich assizes as others would the theatre. But she did not become too puritanical, having her simple Quaker dress made of the finest silk and satin, and she turned from fiction to the writing of improving works. Yet she was still known as 'The Gay Quaker' and was described as 'a very intelligent and pleasant-looking woman, full of life and *malgré* the Quaker's cap, laughed as heartily and talked as much as other people'. In 1851, when she was aged eighty-two, Amelia Opie visited the Great Exhibition in London, where she sighted another old lady in a wheelchair and promptly challenged her to a race.

Another was Harriet Martineau (1820–76), one of eight children of a sternly religious Norwich manufacturer of Huguenot ancestry. Also brought up in the benevolent tradition of the Unitarians, she hoped to become a school-teacher, but poor health (and the lack of senses of taste and smell) combined with increasing deafness to imprison her at home. She had begun writing articles for a Unitarian journal when her father's business collapsed and his sudden death – said to have been caused by shock – was followed by that of her fiancé. But she had already found a cause to occupy her life and energy and devoted herself to the study of social problems and the miseries of the slave trade, publicising them through serious books, novels and journalism. 'I can popularize,' she said, summing up the trade of the journalist, 'while I can neither discover nor invent.'

Harriet Martineau's books, whether heavyweight, like *Illustrations of Political Economy*, fiction, like *Deerbrook*, or books for children – together with her modest charm and calm, amused manner – made her something of a celebrity in London literary circles. But she was a journalist at heart and when cured of an illness by hypnotism, wrote a book about it, *Letters on Mesmerism*. She became one of the first women journalists, joining the *Daily News* as chief leader-writer in 1852; Fleet Street should be proud of her.

Her lifespan overlapped with that of another woman writer who took up the cause of social reform, Mary Mann (1848–

1929). Born in Norwich, married to a gentleman-farmer, she lived on his 800 acres at Shropham, where she found no pastoral idyll. Indeed, she was appalled by rural poverty, by the degradation and brutality it engendered and by the hard struggle faced by many farmers in times of depression. So her novels followed very different themes from those that had romanticised life on the land. Her work was admired by D.H. Lawrence, and Adrian Bell, the East Anglian essayist, wrote that her story-telling 'leaves an epic quality in the mind, a sort of noble rage, which makes for life'. Reform was slow to come but she had helped to bring it nearer.

The Victorian reformers were not all matriarchs. Jeremiah Colman (1830–98) was a boy in Norwich when Elizabeth Fry died but he was brought up to believe that practical good works were as much the duty of the middle class as of the aristocracy. Also nonconformists – the Colmans were Baptists – they, too, were 'in trade' as millers of flour and mustard. The latter, which they had begun to produce at their Stoke Holy Cross mill outside the city at the beginning of the nineteenth century, was what made them famous. Mustard was not only to spice Victorian food but was used in mustard baths, emetics and plasters and Colman was the most famous name in the mustard trade. When Jeremiah took over the business, he moved the mill to Carrow, close to the city, so that mustard could be shipped directly by river and he enlarged it into one of the city's major industries.

But Colman aimed higher than success in trade, exhorting friends and his workers with uplifting exhortations such as 'know then that a humble sphere may be an heroic one; the battle of life may be fought as bravely in a garret, or behind a counter, as on the heights of Alma or the plains of Waterloo'. His own sphere was not to be so humble particularly after his marriage in 1856 to Caroline Cozens Hardy of Letheringsett Hall, whose brother became Lord Justice Cozens Hardy, the Master of the Rolls, who, as will be seen, was to be fixed in the national memory by Sir John Betjeman's poem.

As Colman, a compulsive organiser, became a woolly-bearded patriarch, he sought, like Elizabeth Fry, a wider stage.

He involved himself in local politics and became Mayor of Norwich. The Baptist sect was too small for him and he urged, without success, all the 'Free Churches', of which there were at least eight in Norfolk, to unite. Then, in 1871, he was elected to the House of Commons as Liberal member for Norwich, which he represented for twenty-four years; Gladstone, when Prime Minister, liked to joke in his presence, 'Are we all mustered?' In one field of activity he was all-powerful and that was in the mustard mills of Carrow: 'We don't use the word *can't* at Carrow,' he maintained. There he and his wife founded a penny-a-week school (a halfpenny after the first child) for their workers' families and a free nursing service; it was a welfare state in miniature.

For a man of his energy he was surprisingly relaxed. 'As a public man I must be content with all sorts of criticism and I am not at all disturbed by it even when I think it goes too far,' he said, 'for, on the other hand, I am pretty sure to get more praise than I deserve, so the one may balance the other.' When he died in 1898 his funeral was attended by more than twelve hundred of his workers and the company's great delivery wagons were piled high with wreaths. Colman's Mustard was merged with Reckitts in 1939, but Jeremiah Colman had fathered six children, so continuing the dynasty and its tradition of good works. Colman's of Norwich was finally sold in 1994.

Dissent – both religious and political – had long nudged Norfolk towards a liberal, sometimes radical, stance. The Reform Act of 1832 had divided the county into two constituencies, east and west, each with two Members of Parliament. At first, the Whigs were predominant over the Tories, and then the Liberals took over.

This radical tradition was increasingly followed within the framework of the trade union movement during the nineteenth and twentieth centuries and one of its most effective proponents was Sir George Edwards (1850–1933), who was himself what romantics called a son of toil. Born into a family of farm workers at Marsham, near Aylsham, he himself had been employed as a bird-scarer for a pittance when a child and had been illiterate when he married his forceful wife Charlotte; it was she who inspired him to organise the leaderless farm labourers, whose lot Nelson had once pitied.

Trade unionism had started uneasily in Norfolk because it had grown out of the workers' only means of protest, which had been rioting. Seen by farmers as presenting a threat of further riots, they were understandably hostile to the politicising of their workers by those they considered agitators, although these had often learned oratory in Methodist chapels. Attempts to form an agricultural workers' union initially failed after confrontations with the farmers, but by 1906 they had revived, and George Edwards had been appointed secretary of the Eastern Counties Agricultural Labourers' Union with a membership of 5,000. The Union was affiliated to the Trades Union Congress and its voice was heard in Whitehall as the long, slow campaign to win reasonable conditions for farm workers continued. Edwards's efforts had contributed to the founding of the National Union of Agricultural Workers, of which he became president, when he was recognised as a national leader. In 1920, now aged 70, he was elected Member of Parliament for South Norfolk; ten years later he was knighted for his work in a career which had begun when he was condemned as an agitator and ended with him revered as a statesman of the Labour movement. An annual service of remembrance is still held at his graveside in Fakenham.

A politician of opposing views but also with Norfolk roots was thrown up by the Hoare family and left his mark far beyond Westminster. Samuel Hoare (1880–1959) had been a brilliant scholar at Oxford and, in 1910, was elected to Parliament, where he represented Chelsea for thirty-four years. An imposing man of quiet dignity and deep subtlety, he held a succession of high offices: first as Secretary of State for Air and then India, in which office he was a notable success. This led to his appointment as Foreign Secretary in 1936, as the aggressive intentions of the European dictators were becoming all too apparent. He already knew Mussolini, having, while serving with a military mission in Rome during the First World War, bribed him to support the Allied cause in the newspaper he edited; Hoare had before been entrusted with secret funds for the greasing of potentially friendly palms in Russia and did so with tact and charm.

The Italians were now invading Ethiopia and Hoare made a secret agreement with the French Foreign Minister, Pierre Laval, for the ceding of Ethiopian territory to the Italians to end the fighting and this was approved by the British Government. However, when news leaked of what became notorious as the Hoare-Laval Pact, public reaction was furious; Hoare was accused of appeasing the dictators and had to resign. Yet the next year he was back as First Lord of the Admiralty, then as Home Secretary until the outbreak of the war – surprisingly he favoured the abolition of capital punishment – before being appointed Lord Privy Seal.

Finally, his understanding of the dictators became valuable when the Prime Minister, Winston Churchill, who had opposed him in the past, sent him as ambassador to Spain with the mission of preventing its dictator, General Franco, from allying himself openly with Hitler and Mussolini. This he achieved, again making free use of secret funds and the consequences of his success must remain incalculable. Sir Samuel Hoare became Viscount Templewood and he spent his final years in his native Norfolk at an elegant, single-storey Palladian house he had built before the war near Northrepps, named after his title and decorated with his coat of arms upon a pediment, supported by columns salvaged from the demolished Georgian front of the Bank of England in London. This was expensive and contributed to his wife's complaint of their poverty to Lord Beaverbrook in 1938, at which the press baron paid a total of £6,000 – a large sum at the time – into the Cabinet minister's private account. Thereafter, Lord Templewood was happy to oblige Beaverbrook Newspapers with interviews supporting one or other of their current causes, as I recall from a visit to the Palladian house in the Norfolk woods on behalf of the *Daily Express* and arranged by Lord Beaverbrook, when both men were old but still grinding political axes.

Occasionally, the independent-minded would stray down a political byway. One who did so came from one of the most deeply-rooted of Norfolk families, the Fountaines of Narford. Andrew Fountaine (b. 1921), a direct descendant of Sir Andrew Fountaine, the early eighteenth-century man of affairs and connoisseur, had stood unsuccessfully for parliament as an Independent Conservative in 1950 but veered sharply to the right and became a founder of the National Front. From Narford Hall in the west of the county, where he maintained his inheritance and managed his land, he tried to make his opinions heard. Some of his views about the need for British independence, for the nurturing of British culture, would have attracted wide support, but his approach was not one of gentle persuasion. His solution was an aggressive nationalism, including the repatriation of immigrants and a refusal to acknowledge the nation's reduced status. It was sad that a man of such energy had not chosen a path that could have been validated by the electorate. Yet he has been, in the tradition of Tom Paine, a man ready to stand up and proclaim ideas he knew to be widely unpopular.

Political ideas generated in Norfolk have usually grown out of an urge to change patterns of living and working in the county itself. But occasionally they burst the frontiers of county and country to take global effects through the medium of what was then the British Empire. Two Norfolk imperialists, who generated such ideas, were Sir Rider Haggard (1856–1925) and Frank Brayne (1882–1952).

The former, the sixth of the squire of West Bradenham's seven sons, had alone been deemed unworthy of an expensive education; he was sent to Ipswich Grammar School and various crammers before being packed off to Africa as an unpaid aide to Sir Henry Bulwer of Heydon, who had been appointed Lieutenant-Governor of Natal. In Africa, he also worked as a law officer and then as an ostrich farmer, returning to marry the heiress to an estate at Ditchingham in the south-east of the county, which he eventually farmed himself. He became most famous, of course, as a hugely successful novelist of boundless imagination. He himself did not, however, regard his life's work as the creation of She-Who-Must-Be-Obeyed and other over-heated fantasies, for Rider Haggard was rooted in the real world of farming and manual labour. His concern about Norfolk agriculture became translated into a concept of a global Anglo-Saxon empire through his ability to harness imagination to practicalities.

Haggard took the management of his estate at Ditchingham very seriously as a duty of stewardship and he was deeply disturbed at the drift of farming families from the land. 'If high civilisation necessitates a flight from the villages, then it is of a truth that broad road which leads to the destruction of advanced peoples,' he believed. The answer was to improve conditions of work on the land and he advocated more generous pay and forms of social welfare. But he also sought to entice new blood from the towns into the country, although he realised that it might be two or three generations before the urban poor could be transformed into sturdy rural stock.

Rider Haggard stood for election as Unionist (or Conservative) candidate for East Norfolk in the general election of 1895; tall, loose-limbed, aggressively bearded and a passionate orator, he fought a hard campaign and nearly won the seat. However, some of his ideas would have appealed to Tom Paine for amongst them was the compulsory purchase and redistribution of land to found a new class of smallholding yeoman farmer. Although a churchwarden of his Church of England parish, he became friends with 'General' William Booth of the Salvation Army and discussed with him training schemes in farming for unemployed townsmen. This led directly to his plans for settlement in the Empire, firstly of such urban recruits and then, during the First World War, of ex-servicemen and their families when peace returned.

Initially, Haggard hoped to implement such a scheme through the Dominions Royal Commission, which studied the economic future of the English-speaking dominions and which he joined in 1912. But he had always had reservations about the suitability of townsmen for country life and, after 1914, increasingly warmed to the idea of the survivors of the war's fighting men being rewarded – like Roman legionaries, or Cromwell's Ironsides – with land and a secure future. But in the midst of the war, the Government was too busy to concern itself with post-war planning and the Dominions Royal Commission had been wound up. However, the Royal Colonial Institute sponsored his scheme and, in 1916, he set out to tour the Dominions, seeking support for post-war settlement. In innumerable speeches throughout South Africa, Australia, New Zealand and Canada, the famous author with the glittering eye and bristling beard, asked his huge audiences, 'What is our Empire?' In Tasmania, he declared,

> It covers fully one-fourth of the globe and is held by about 60,000,000 white people, of whom 40,000,000 dwell in the United Kingdom. It is just all that we can do to hold the Empire with that population . . . Now is the opportunity for the Empire to try to secure for that land . . . the finest settlers in the world – men who have been thoroughly disciplined, who know what stress and danger mean and who know how to face opposition of every kind . . . Then there is the debt we owe to our sailors and soldiers . . .

The alternative, he told them, was the occupation of that land by Asians and he warned: 'In a day to come – say fifty years hence – the countless yellow races, armed to the teeth and practically unconquerable, may be in a position to do what Germany has done, but with better success, that is to attempt to obtain the supremacy of the world'.

His lone crusade was a remarkable success and Dominion governments voted him vast tracts of land for the post-war settlement he advocated. But on the day he returned to London in July 1916, news had broken of the first great slaughter of the Battle of the Somme, and from that moment both the Government and the press were too preoccupied to concern themselves with post-war planning. Haggard won his knighthood but not his crusade, although it did eventually bear some fruit in a limited amount of subsidised emigration to the Dominions. But there was not to be the Pole-to-Pole Anglo-Saxon empire he had imagined.

Sir Rider may possibly have met Frank Brayne and, if he did, would have recognised him as an enlightened fellow-imperialist. Both were muscular Christians, dedicated to the concept that the enlightened should help the backward. Brayne and his wife, Iris, were both rooted in Norfolk and steeped in its traditions, but their reforming zeal was focused on countryside that could not have been more different: the Punjab. Yet Brayne worked in the Indian Civil Service at a period when the 'Jewel in the Crown' did not seem much more distant from Norfolk than Cornwall. Probably most of the educated inhabitants of the county were related to, or knew, somebody who worked in India as an administrator, soldier, businessman, doctor or missionary; even the less-affluent often knew a soldier or sailor who had served there. Sun-burned Norfolkmen on leave would tell stories about the mysteries, dangers, beauties, plagues and the sheer difference of India from all that was familiar at home.

One such was Frank Brayne as I remember him. He was impossible to forget: a tall, erect, muscular man with a deceptively donnish appearance imparted by gold, round-rimmed spectacles and a little, clipped, grey moustache, he radiated energy and ideas. His house at Ashill was furnished with savage weaponry and the stuffed, or flayed remains of wild animals he had killed: a crocodile's skin down the banisters of the long staircase; a leopardskin rug on the hearth.

'Did you shoot the leopard, sir?' I once asked.

'No, I strangled it,' he replied, explaining how the wounded beast had sprung at him, knocked his gun from his grasp and they had rolled, locked in hand-to-paw combat down a ravine, from which he had emerged the victor.

But Brayne's fame rested on far more positive action. The son of a rector of Kirstead – and nephew of Lord Lugard, a Governor-General of Nigeria – he had been introduced to his future wife, Iris Goble (also a child of a Norfolk rectory and inspired by the same indoctrination as himself) by my mother. It was typical of her breed, that Iris Brayne should take India in her stride, bringing up five children in the wilds and involving herself in her husband's work to such an extent that a senior British administrator remarked after meeting the

Braynes that they reminded him of a railway line: 'two shining strips of steel, heading inexorably towards their destination'.

Brayne saw himself as a bringer of civilisation to backward peoples and would not have been ashamed to be described as a paternalist. This attitude has, of course, been mocked but, held by the son of a rector and a graduate of Cambridge University, suddenly set down amidst the squalor and disease of central India, is understandable. He brought to his task the same enthusiasm of the muscular Christian that he would have brought to a Norfolk parish had he followed his father into the Church of England; he wrote books with titles like *The Boy Scout in the Village* and also became the champion spearer of Indian wild pigs from horse-back.

The doctrine of self-help had become a Victorian doctrine amongst English-speaking Christians since Samuel Smiles had written his book *Self Help* (in the year of the Indian Mutiny, as it happened), and it fell on particularly fertile ground amongst the Low Church and nonconformist congregations of Norfolk. As Brayne saw it, it was no good nannying the villagers of the Punjab, they must be taught and encouraged to help themselves. So, in 1920, he unleashed upon the 700,000 inhabitants of the backward Gurgaon region east of Delhi an exercise in self-help known as 'village uplift' and called 'The Gurgaon Experiment'.

With dauntless zeal, the Braynes set about teaching the villagers practical husbandry, housekeeping and hygiene in a crusade that lasted seven years and became famous throughout India. Being near Delhi, the project was frequently visited by the Viceroy and his important guests, when Brayne showed himself a master of public relations. Some found him impossibly overbearing and self-absorbed. 'We talked entirely of the Braynes and their doings,' noted one. 'What a simple-minded egoist he is and how full of self-praise. "No one in India can stick a pig as I can", etc. And how dogmatic. Just as I was going, he presented me with a pamphlet on manure pits and a poster of his sixteen commandments to hang upon my poor innocent wall.' Brayne sometimes realised that he had been carried away by his own enthusiasm and would stop and say, 'I must bury my trumpeter', meaning that he had blown his own trumpet too long and loud.

Yet such self-absorbed dedication is often the mark of the crusader and such was Brayne. To claim, as a critical biographer has done, that his life's work was wasted because the village uplift campaign collapsed once he had left the Gurgaon, missed the point that no positive action is wholly wasted and that it might have continued had he found a successor of similar idealism and drive. On his return to Norfolk in 1946 he planned another form of village uplift. Shocked by the number of retired, fit but inactive men in the Norfolk villages, he gave an interview to the *Daily Mail* explaining how he had bought fruit orchards at Ashill while on leave from India, planted trees and left them in the charge of a local farmer so that, on his return, he had a mature fruit farm awaiting him. It might have been more difficult for others to emulate him than he suggested but his overall message was simple and clear: plan for the future. It had been thus in India.

Although Norfolk lacked the socialist foundations of the industrial counties, it maintained its liberal views through most of the twentieth century. When the Whigs' successors, the Liberals, collapsed as a political force in the 1920s, the county turned towards the Labour Party. Yet the electorate remained independent-minded and in 1979 swung to the Conservatives in the first of Mrs Thatcher's electoral victories.

Among the other successful women politicians thrown up by the long years of Conservative rule was a native of Norfolk, who represented her county in Parliament: Gillian Shephard of North Walsham (b. 1947). A former school-teacher, schools inspector and member of the Norfolk County Council, she became Member of Parliament for Norfolk South-West in 1987. Brisk and efficient but friendly and approachable, she soon showed herself to be of ministerial material, as Employment Secretary, Agriculture Minister and, in 1994, Secretary of State for Education, a post for which she was well-prepared. The other politician of her generation to emerge from the county was also a woman and took her place on the opposite side of the House of Commons. Margaret Beckett (née Jackson; b. 1943) came from Norwich but represented Lincoln (1974–9) for the Labour Party and Derby South since 1982, a year later becoming Deputy Leader. On the sudden death of John Smith in 1994, she became Acting Leader until Tony Blair and John Prescott were elected to the leadership later in the year.

There were originators of ideas among the later settlers, too. Amongst these were the philosopher Edward de Bono (b. 1933), the prophet of 'lateral thinking', who chose to live in the splendid Georgian house, Cranmer Hall, near Fakenham.

The saviour of another great Norfolk house – and of others elsewhere – deserves to be remembered as a man of ideas: Kit Martin (b. 1947), the architect. When the colossal Gunton Hall, the seat of the Harbord family since the eighteenth century, came on the market in 1980 it seemed that it could only be used as a school but was probably too vast even for that. Then it was acquired by Kit Martin, who, with skill and sensitivity, converted it into a complex of twenty self-contained houses and flats while retaining the cohesive looks of a single Georgian mansion.

After working in Scotland and the Midlands, Martin, who himself lived at Gunton, again turned his attention to Norfolk in 1994 for the conversion of the old Naval Hospital, which had been built at Great Yarmouth during the Napoleonic wars. Later converted into barracks and then used as a mental hospital, the four arcaded blocks of grey brick, each twenty-nine bays long, were to be divided into fifty houses, so preserving the handsome Georgian complex and, perhaps, enhancing the social composition of the town.

The generation of ideas through the schools of Norfolk was crowned in 1963 by the foundation of the University of East Anglia set around Earlham Hall, once the home of the Gurneys; its grim but functional new buildings designed by Sir Denys Lasdun. There the importance of the region's history was stressed by the setting up of the Centre for East Anglian Studies, which at once set about compiling and publishing a two-volume *Bibliography of Norfolk History*, pointing the way to the study of what the Victorians would have called its highways and byways and the nooks and crannies of its past.

VI
Arts

When the wind rattles the tiles and roars in the chimney, it is time to tell stories. In the Norfolk of my youth – in the second quarter of the twentieth century – these were sometimes ghost stories: the Grey Lady met in the herb garden of a Tudor mansion; the RAF pilot forever playing fives in the court at Bircham Newton, to which he never returned from a flight; even Old Shuck, the phantom hound of the salt-marshes. They were sometimes stories of eccentric landowners, or coast-guards and smugglers; poachers and gamekeepers. The cast was large; the variety infinite.

The earliest stories had come down from the time before history was recorded. There are no brooding hills in Norfolk such as produced Border ballads but the wide horizons and great skies must have invited moody reflection. Many of the earliest stories were expunged by invaders, who slaughtered those entrusted with the oral history of the tribe, or burned the monastery libraries. Later old manuscripts were swept into bonfires, or the stories simply forgotten. Those that survived were, however, passed on and sometimes improved upon.

Such stories were repeated in castle keeps and hovels; in country house libraries, rectory studies, front parlours and tap-rooms, gently embellished along the way. Sometimes they were turned into fiction by such as M. R. James, or L. P. Hartley, or recorded by the scholar, or county historian, most notably by R. W. Ketton-Cremer. Occasionally fiction almost became fact, as when Russell Thorndike, in old age, would enjoy inventing legends, which some, at first, believed. 'What's behind that blocked-up door?' a visitor would ask in the parlour of the former pub in Foulsham, where he latterly lived. The reply, accompanied by a transfixing stare, would be: 'Not so long ago, they did open that door and do you know what they found beyond? Four Georgian gentlemen at cards.' Norfolk has had its storytellers as well as its writers, and a few poets; in another dimension, it had its artists, too.

The first writer of note in his own time, with a reputation that has survived the centuries, was Sir Thomas Browne (1605–82), whose bronze statue gazes thoughtfully upon the shopping crowds in the commercial centre of Norwich. Otherwise Browne is one of the forgotten writers, despite references to his 'rich English prose', read only by scholars delving into the intellectual strivings of the seventeenth century.

He was a doctor, born in London and not settling in Norwich until he was thirty-two. He was taken up by county families – notably the Harbords – who recorded his prescriptions, which make comic, or even rather charming reading, like 'Doctor Browne's Purge of Damask Roses': 'Take 50 Roses and infuse them all night in a wine pint of claryfiyed Whey, put in 4 Spoonfulls of White Wine and half a Spoonfull of Carraway Seeds, in the morning make it ready to boyle and strain it and put in 3 Spoonfuls of Sirrop of Violets'.

Like other physicians of his day, Browne had remarkably eclectic interests. When the diarist John Evelyn visited him, he recorded that his house and garden were 'a paradise and cabinet or rarities . . . especially medails, books, plants and natural things . . . eggs of all the foule and birds he could procure, that country (especially the promontory of Norfolck) being frequented by severall kinds, which seldom or never go farther into the land, as cranes, storkes, eagles and a variety of water-foule'. Indeed Dr Browne kept a stork and an eagle, which he fed on cats and puppies. In preserving bottles were grotesque deep-sea fish, dredged up in Yarmouth fishermen's nets, and, amongst his curiosties, 'giants teeth', found at Earsham, which turned out to have belonged to an ox.

His literary reputation rested upon philosophical musings on religions and the human predicament. His first work *Religio Medici* was published in 1642 and was talked about much as Professor Stephen Hawking's theories are today. More reflections following an archaeological find prompted

'*Urne-Buriall, or A Discourse of the Sepuchrall Urnes lately found in Norfolk*'. His interests included natural history and horticulture and, amongst his other books, was a curious work *The Garden,* which examined only the period between the Garden of Eden and Persian gardens at the time of Cyrus.

Browne was a Royalist during the Civil War and was knighted when King Charles II visited Norwich after the Restoration; indeed his trim moustache and tuft of beard gave him something of the look of a Cavalier. He was, apparently, a kindly man with an enquiring mind, who preached religious tolerance. But this did not extend to witchcraft and it was due to his recommendation, following his study of the evidence, that two old women were hanged as witches. He also adopted more rational means of undermining belief in magic with a simple experiment. The peacock had long been regarded as a symbol of immortality and St Augustine was credited with the belief that its flesh was therefore incorruptible. So Browne hung up a dead peacock long enough to prove that that was not so.

Sadly, in the next century, Norfolk failed to attract Horace Walpole (1717–97), although he finally inherited the splendours of Houghton Hall and was buried in its church in the depths of the countryside where he felt so ill at ease. This witty, sophisticated man, with his ready smile, quick eyes and sharp, inquisitive nose, was at home in London and at Strawberry Hill, his Gothick mansion in the fashionable outer suburb of Twickenham, but disliked mixing with those he described as 'roast beef fashioned in human form' in Norfolk. He was also antipathetic towards his nephew, the dissolute, unstable George Walpole, third Earl of Orford, who lived with his mistress, Patty, a former maidservant at Houghton, and so had no direct heir to inherit the title and Houghton. But by then Colen Campbell's *palazzo* in the rolling, wooded country east of King's Lynn was, together with its estate, in a shocking state of neglect.

George was the grandson of the great Sir Robert Walpole, Prime Minister to King George I and builder of Houghton; his character was summed up by his sharp-eyed uncle, Horace:

'He has more of the easy, genuine air of quality than ever you saw' but was 'the most selfish man in the world . . . it is impossible not to love him when one sees him: impossible to esteem him when one thinks on him!' A man of fashion, he drank and philandered without passion, devoting his enthusiasm to field sports and gambling: not only hunting and racing but cock-fighting and bull-baiting. Once he arranged a race of five turkeys against five geese from Norwich to London. He harnessed two pairs of red deer to a phaeton and drove about the country roads until chancing upon a pack of foxhounds, which immediately chased him until they happened to pass their own kennels, and, from force of habit, entered and an alert kennelman shut the gate behind them. Yet however much his sophisticated uncle might despise him, Norfolk people loved his dottiness, particularly as he had aged into the sort of squire caricatured by Rowlandson, on the borderline between rural rake and eccentric. Then, in 1791, his beloved Patty died and he followed her a month later, passing the earldom to the dilettante squire of Twickenham.

Horace Walpole had become Member of Parliament for two Norfolk constituencies, Castle Rising and then King's Lynn, but had kept away from Houghton until, in 1773, during one of his nephew's bouts of insanity, he was summoned to put his house and estate in some sort of order. There he found Sir Robert's great creation 'half a ruin . . . the two great staircases exposed to all weathers, every room in the wings rotting with wet, the ceiling of the gallery in danger, the chancel of the church unroofed . . . the park half covered with nettles and weeds, the walls in ruin . . . mortgages swallowing the estate . . . a crew of banditti were harboured in the house'. Happily, if surprisingly, Horace was efficient and, after sacking the surplus staff and selling most of the horses and hounds, he put the house and estate on a sound footing by the time George recovered at the end of the year. The tribulations of Houghton were far from over, and George sold his grandfather's collection of paintings to the Empress Catherine of Russia.

Horace now found himself 'the poorest Earl in England' and master of Houghton, where even the stone steps leading to the *piano nobile* had been given away (finally to be replaced nearly two centuries later by Lady Cholmondeley – formerly Sybil Sassoon – who did so much to restore Houghton to its full, original grandeur). The new Lord Orford was now in his seventies and no longer capable of taking charge of his inheritance, preferring to stay at his London house in Berkeley Square and the warmer weather at Strawberry Hill. It was at Twickenham that he died in 1797, returning to Norfolk in the hearse that bore him to join the other Walpoles in their vault. Circumstances and inclination had deprived Norfolk of the attentions of a great writer.

But as well as his wit, Horace Walpole left a surprising legacy in a Houghton restored. A year after his death, a traveller, Samuel Pratt, described his arrival there: 'Till we get within about two miles of Houghton, a contracted kind of scenery prevails but then it is that more spacious fields, ample pastures and extended woodlands, with a road broadening at your feet and foliage arching over your head, announce something extraordinary. By the imposing alternation of these, you enter upon the long-celebrated domain of the Walpoles.'

Norfolk could claim as partly its own several transient writers who briefly settled there over the next two centuries. The poet William Cowper (1731–1800) only spent the last five years of his life in Norfolk, dying in East Dereham. There he wrote *The Castaway*, which is now forgotten, so Norfolk can claim no part in the creation of his famous quotations, 'Variety's the very spice of life', 'the cups that cheer but do not inebriate', 'God made the country and man made the town' and 'England, for all thy faults, I love thee still'; nor, indeed, of his best-remembered verse *The Ballad of John Gilpin*. Even so, Dereham commemorates him with a stained-glass window in its church.

Several Norfolkmen whose writings are preserved in print were not, however, authors but letter-writers (like the Pastons), or diarists (like Parson Woodforde and Silas Neville). The latter (1741–1840) was a man of means – although he lost much of his inheritance at cards and on the turf – and, despite the fact that he lived in London for a while and travelled extensively, his natural home was in Norwich, where he ended his days. His diary (part of which was published in 1950) gives a lively impression of the second half of the eighteenth century as it appeared to a privileged, alert man in early middle age.

There is for example the view of the fiercely-fought general election campaign as seen in Norwich: 'Mon. Apr. 5. Election Day. A great bustle in the Market; the poll continued till 7 o'clock. A brilliant appearance of ladies at the windows engaged my attention more than the different success of the candidates. I was sometimes in the Market, the scene of action, and sometimes at a window, where I could see all the contending parties.' And next day, 'Another scene of anarchy and bustle in the Hall in St. Andrews . . . A fair on Tombland for toys, etc., full of Beaux and belles before dinner and tag-rag and bobtail in the evening.' Then the following day, watching the new members 'chaired' round Castle Hill and the Market: 'A number of fine country girls on the Hill, etc., and a great show of beauty at the windows of the Market Place . . . In the afternoon, an air balloon dismissed from Bunn's garden; saw it ascend from my own house.'

Neville visited Holkham Hall in August, 1788, to dine with Thomas Coke, then aged thirty-four. 'Went on what they call the home circuit with some of the ladies and gentlemen,' he noted.

This is a little tour to see the grounds, different vistas, etc. The park, when the plan is completed, will be 11 miles round.

Rode on horseback . . . This is one of their public days. 28 at dinner. Two courses of 26 or 28 dishes . . . 1st. course: Principal dishes, a variety of soups, stewed carp and other fish, all other made dishes, one very good. Ox's palates stewed and rolled up with small lettuces between. 2nd. course: Haunch of venison, Leverets, Rabbits, Pastry, Blomange, Jelly, Oysters . . . Dined in the Statue Gallery . . . Style of life: An immense house, an immense establishment, etc. A great deal of company . . . little time for domestic enjoyment and none for reading. An uncomfortable life!

Norfolk bred a more sophisticated diarist – and novelist – in Fanny Burney (1752–1840). Born in the town then called Lynn Regis, the daughter of the celebrated musician Dr

Charles Burney, then organist to St Margaret's, she followed
her parents to London when she was eighteen but sometimes
returned to Norfolk. As a girl, her feelings about life in Lynn
were mixed. On the one hand, she recorded her pleasure in
country walks before breakfast when 'the fields near Lynn . . .
are, in my eyes, particularly charming at that time in the
morning – the sun is warm and not sultry and there is a scarce a
soul to be seen. Near the capital I should not dare indulge
myself in this delightful manner for fear of robbers.' On the
other, she found social life petty and restrictive, complaining,

> Such a set of tittle tattle, prittle prattle visitants! Oh dear, I am so sick of
> the ceremony and fuss of these fall lall people! So much dressing – chit
> chat – complimentary nonsense – in short a Country Town is my
> detestation – all the conversation is scandal, all the attention, dress and
> *almost* all the heart, folly, envy and censoriousness. A City or a village are
> the only places which I can think can be comfortable, for a Country
> Town, I think, has all the bad qualities, without one of the good ones, of
> both.

So Fanny Burney outgrew Lynn Regis, while her father,
who had become friends with the neighbouring landowners,
was to become organist at the Royal Hospital, Chelsea, when
one of them, Lord Townshend of Raynham, was the
Governor. Fanny, now famous as the author of *Evelina*,
Cecilia and other novels, married a French émigré, General
d'Arblay, and took her place in the fashionable literary world
far from Lynn.

Captain Frederick Marryat (1792–1848) also spent only the
last five years in Norfolk, although he had owned his house,
the Manor, and a thousand acres at Langham for thirteen years
before settling there. A Londoner by birth, Marryat joined the
Royal Navy a year after Trafalgar, fought in the war with
France and later commanded the naval squadron – including
steamers – in the Burma campaign of 1824. Successful as he
was at sea, it was as a novelist that he became famous. His first
book *Frank Mildmay* – a vivid, cynical story about a self-
aware, self-critical naval officer – was written while he was
still serving. But it was too honest and realistic to be well
received, and he turned to novels of action and humour; and

these were enormously successful, notably *Peter Simple* and *Mr Midshipman Easy*. Jaded with the life of a celebrity in London, Wimbledon and Brighton, in 1839 he moved to his house in Norfolk, where, as his daughter put it, he

> tried very hard to be a regular farmer. He tried to drain the Cley saltmarshes; he built model cottages and instituted model pigsties; both cottagers and pigs proved averse to anything like progressive movement. He ... put on gaiters and mounting a rough, thickset pony (called Dumpling) rode about from dyke to ditch and from ditch to dyke, standing patiently for hours whilst he watched his men drain Fox's Covert, or exorcise the will-o'the-wisp from the Decoy Meadow; but for all that he was a farmer in theory only and not in practice.

Perhaps it was his old shrewdness as a commander of rough men that prompted him to appoint the local poacher as his gamekeeper.

He tried to run the Manor like a ship of the line, stowing his sea chest in the hall and going to immense trouble to ensure that all his sixteen clocks struck together; he built a rock garden in the shape of a ship's poop, so that he could pace to and fro as had been his custom.

A robust, convivial man, with a broad, handsome face, and well-built, he enjoyed company but, beyond a Lieutenant Thomas of the Coastguard at Blakeney, found a shortage of cronies. He continued writing, mostly for children, and his *The Children of the New Forest* in fact reflects life in Norfolk rather than Hampshire. He hankered after the company of his naval and literary friends, particularly Charles Dickens, and the artists Landseer and Maclise, and he would invite them to Langham for the shooting and they would invite him to dine in London; yet because of the distance and poor communications they seldom met.

Finally, disappointment over the failure of the Admiralty to provide an expected pension was followed by the news of the death of his son Frederick, also a naval officer, in the wreck of HMS *Avenger* in the Mediterranean. He had had two sons in the Navy and Frederick took after Jack Easy, the hero of *Mr Midshipman Easy*, in that, when at home, 'like all midshipmen he turns the house upside down and very much disturbs the economy and well regulating of a family', as his father put it. But it must have been gratifying to hear that, when his ship was lost in December, 1847, 'the last that was seen of your fine son was on deck, upbraiding in his jocular manner some people who were frightened, when a sea swept over the ship and took him with it'.

The news bowed Marryat with grief. As ill-health overtook him, he would dictate stories to his daughters and they would bring him bunches of pinks and roses from his garden. Then, as his mind wandered, he would hold imaginary conversation with Dickens and his old shipmates while staring out of the tall windows at his garden, ripe with summer. Finally, he died in his sleep in August, 1848, and was buried in the churchyard at Langham. He had been a remarkable link between ages: remembering the arrival of the news of Trafalgar; fighting under sail; hobnobbing with the great Victorian literary figures. Only one of his four sons survived him and he died young, though one of his seven daughters lived until 1932.

While Captain Marryat, like most other writers in Norfolk, was migratory, alighting on passage or to find seclusion and rest, George Borrow (1803–81) was a true Norfolkman and made the county his base for expeditions. He was born at East Dereham, his mother a farmer's daughter from Dumpling Green, who became an actress and had caught the eye of the Cornish sergeant-major of the West Norfolk Militia. Educated at Norwich School, he lived in the city – his tiny house survives, tucked away in a close of modern houses just off Cow Hill – and, later, at Great Yarmouth, Oulton and across the Suffolk border in Lowestoft.

Borrow is remembered for his sympathy for, and under-standing of, gypsies, whose Romany language he spoke. One friend, meeting him in the year of Marryat's death, went walking with him and wrote,

> We fell in with some gypsies and I heard the speech of Egypt, which sounded wondrously like a medley of broken Spanish and dog Latin. Borrow's face, lighted up by the red turf fire of the tent, was worth looking at. He is ashy-white now . . . but twenty years ago, when his hair was like a raven's wing, he must have been hard to discriminate from a

born Bohemian. Borrow is best on the tramp: if you can walk 4½ miles per hour . . . and can walk 15 of them at a stretch . . . then he will talk Iliads of adventures even better than his printed ones.

Borrow spoke Romany but such dialogue around a gypsy camp fire is not easy to imagine. In his novel *Lavengro*, he described a philosophical conversation with a gypsy camped on Mousehold Heath above Norwich:

> 'Life is sweet, brother.'
> 'Do you think so?'
> 'Think so! There's night and day, brother, both sweet things; sun, moon and stars, brother, all sweet things; there's likewise a wind on the heath. Life is very sweet, brother; who would wish to die?'

The gypsy says that any Romany would want to live for ever.

> 'In sickness, Jasper?'
> 'There's the sun and the stars, brother.'
> 'In blindness, Jasper?'
> 'There's the wind on the heath; if only I could feel that, I would gladly live for ever.'

Borrow's wanderlust took him far beyond Norfolk, to Spain as an agent for the British Bible Society. He was there during a civil war and this, together with descriptions of his travels, are the background to his book *The Bible in Spain*. He was a strange, moody man, who suffered from fits of depression but seems to have found relief on those great walks under the wide, windy skies of Norfolk. Inappropriately, he is not buried in a lonely country churchyard but, together with his wife, in the marble necropolis of West Brompton Cemetery in London.

George Borrow was followed in his own lifetime by another Norfolkman with a taste for the exotic, although Borrow's gypsies were garden gnomes compared with the imagined creatures of Rider Haggard (1856–1925). His novels, *King Solomon's Mines* and *She*, thrilled their readers, most of them young and unable to appreciate that, in the latter book, the strange, undefinable excitement was, in fact, erotic. In his fifty-eight novels, he only occasionally drew on his experience as the son of a Norfolk squire and then, a squire himself, on his experience as a farmer. In *Colonel Quarich, V.C.*, he wrote of a Norfolk family with the gentry defending themselves against the grasping *nouveaux riches*, but mostly he is up and away in lost civilisations, Zululand, Ancient Egypt and elsewhere in the past; the bloodier the better.

Once he combined the country-house life he knew with his fantasies, when in *The Ancient Allan*, his hero Allan Quatermain, loosely modelled on himself, is invited to his beautiful hostess's private museum to take a drug, which will waft them back to Ancient Egypt. The inspiration of this was a real country house between King's Lynn and Swaffham, Didlington Hall. This vast mansion with its woodland, lakes and follies was owned by the Amherst family, which had a taste for the bizarre far outstripping that of Sir Thomas Browne and filled a large private museum added to their house. It was there amongst the exotic jumble of treasures and knick-knacks from the Nile to Florence, the Louvre to Babylon, that the young Rider Haggard was shown the little, wooden funerary figure from an Egyptian tomb with a sweetly serene expression on its painted face. This, it is said, combined with a childhood memory of an evil-faced rag doll in the toy-cupboard at his childhood home, Bradenham Hall, with which the nurserymaid used to frighten the children, came together to inspire the character of She-Who-Must-Be-Obeyed.

One Edwardian visitor recalled visiting the museum, bemused by the splendiferous hoard, and seeing that

> in the long, lofty hall sit in solitary state a row of basalt figures, holding in their hands the symbolic key of the Nile. For thousands of years, these cat-headed goddesses were worshipped by the Egyptians; they have survived dynasties and empires to look down complacently on the trees which the Prince of Wales and the Duke of Edinburgh planted when they visited Didlington . . .

Rider Haggard, the novelist (and also farmer, social reformer and imperialist) was obsessed by the land he worked and the mystery of its past. 'How many dead hands have tilled that fallow, or mown that pasture?' he mused. 'And the land itself? Scarcely changed, I believe.' There he wrote many of the books that made him famous – fantasies, historical novels and novels of contemporary social life – and here, too, he wrote *A Farmer's Year*, a marvellous rag-bag of stories and ideas compiled during 1898, and reflecting his hectic imagination more clearly than the work of the farm.

Haggard was often abroad – particularly in Africa and, latterly, as a crusading imperialist, touring the British Empire – but always returned to the county that saw his birth and to his house on the low escarpment above the Waveney Valley. 'I have travelled a great way about the world in my time and studied much scenery,' he wrote,

> but I do not remember anything more quietly and consistently beautiful than this view . . . For the most part of the year the plain below is golden with gorse, but it is not on this alone that the sight depends for beauty, or on the green of the meadows and the winding river edged with lush marshes that in spring are spotted by yellow marigolds and purple with myriads of cuckoo flowers. They all contribute to it, as do the grazing cattle, the gabled distant roofs and the church spires, but I think that the prospect owes its peculiar charm to the constant changes of light which sweep across its depths. At every season of the year, at every hour of the day it is beautiful, but always with a different beauty.

Here, in the churchyard of St Mary's, his only son, who died at the age of nine, breaking his father's heart, is buried and here at Ditchingham House – known locally as Mustard Pot Hall because of the yellow lichen on its roof – his three daughters were born. The youngest, Lilias (1892–1968), also became a writer, catching the flavour of Norfolk even more acutely than her father in her study of a poacher, *I Walked by Night*, and her essays on country life, notably those written when she was living at Blakeney, have a particular potency:

> I was down on the salt-marshes the other day in the still, shimmering warmth of a hot afternoon. The tide had run far out, leaving mile after mile of opalescent mud and beyond, great stretches of yellow sand away to the horizon, where a thin line of breakers fringed the brilliant blue of the deep sea. It was very quiet . . . A lark rose sometimes, let fall a few broken phrases and dropped again into the bents. A tern wandered past in wavering, inconsequent flight, checked at a sight of some flickering shadow in the thin stream of translucent water still running down the

centre of the creek from the river, fanned with shivering wings and then, half closing them, dived like a stone dropping and flickered away again on its airy path . . .

Sometimes she collaborated with another writer, Henry Williamson (1897–1977). Like Sir Rider Haggard, Williamson farmed in Norfolk and wrote about it. Like Haggard he had strong political views, but whereas the older man was an enlightened imperialist with what he called 'a cross-bench mind', Williamson was a supporter of Sir Oswald Mosley's British Union of Fascists. Like others so inclined, he was a product of what they knew as the Great War and was determined that politicians should never be again allowed to create such a catastrophe, relying instead on what he saw as the comradeship of the trenches (as did a former German soldier, Adolf Hitler, who lacked Williamson's essential humanity). When Williamson bought his farm at Stiffkey in 1937, the European Fascists and Nazis were already alarming the British and Hitler's ranting, threatening oratory was broadcast through wireless sets in remotest Norfolk.

So, although Williamson was already famous as the author of the brilliant novel of animal life, *Tarka the Otter*, written in Devon a decade before, he was unpopular and distrusted, particularly as war threatened, when he was seen as a potential collaborator, if not a potential enemy spy. He was, of course, neither but lacked mature judgement; he had the eyes of a defensive, intelligent adolescent – such as he had been when swept into war as a young soldier – still wild and wary but staring from a middle-aged face. His account of his two years in Norfolk, *The Story of a Norfolk Farm*, remains a record of agricultural depression and a segment in the life of a strange, talented but ultimately sad writer. This book is a touching evocation of a rural Norfolk that is now gone but it does give flashes of recognisable scenes, notably of the weather. One winter day, for example, he is out walking with his young son and he writes,

> Seldom have I seen such a louring mass of clouds. We hastened on, and were half-way home when the edge of the cloud reached us. A bitter twisting wind blew the snow into our eyes; the thorn hedge and the line of

furze bushes between the marsh and the fields were dissolved in our sight. We walked forward with heads bowed, eyes half-shut and holding hands. Two miles to go . . . On we went, the left side of our faces, exposed to the wind and the prickle-drive of snow, feeling as though the flesh had been rived with a knife and the bone exposed . . .

Silently, in a world of white, we crossed the fields . . . and so to the village street, glimmering in star-light; and we saw again the small familiar yellow squares and rectangles of the windows. The snow had stopped, the wind was quiet. No noise or headlights of cars; it was an old English village again. I wanted to take the silence, and the rare peacefulness, to myself, and leaned against a flint wall to think back into the past . . .

Williamson was not a Norfolkman and never took to East Anglia, unlike two of his contemporaries, R.W. Ketton-Cremer (1906–69) and L. P. Hartley (1895–1977). They were two large, lumbering bachelors but very different in temperament. Windham Ketton-Cremer, the fastidious squire of Felbrigg Hall, blended with its mellow magnificence, its picture-galleries, its rococo jewel-box of a room, built by a Georgian forebear to house his souvenirs of the Grand Tour, called the Cabinet, and its Gothick library. It was here that he wrote his books about Norfolk worthies – scholars and rakes, clerics and soldiers, Cavaliers and Roundheads, many of them bred in houses such as his own; indeed, an autobiographical chapter could have taken its place in any of those works with titles such as *A Norfolk Gallery*, *Norfolk Portraits* and *Norfolk Assembly*. A ponderous man, observing the conventions of his youth, he became a sad, solitary figure in the great house, built by long-dead landowners, with whose families he was so proud to be linked, and preserved by himself. His handsome, dashing younger brother had been killed fighting in Crete during the Second World War, so there was no one to inherit the house and lands except the nation through the National Trust. He himself, the squire and historian of Felbrigg, wrote its history, ending with the words,

It is scarcely twenty years since my brother died in Crete, when we waited for news of him, and heard none, in just such another spring. Day after day the verdure increases – the brilliance of the beeches, the endlessly diversified green of the oaks, the chestnuts richly flowering, the reluctant ashes, the hawthorns 'white again, in spring, with voluptuary sweetness'.

As always, the plovers cry in the meadows. As always, the cold wind sweeps in from the sea.

It was left to a neighbour, Michael Riviere (b.1919), to describe Ketton-Cremer and do so in verse:

> Families have no beginning, but can end,
> Though 350 armigerous years
> Brighten the vellum. But life may descend
> Obliquely, and a score of Norfolk squires
> Are summed up here into fresh dimension
> That can progenerate outside the reach
> Of country gossip and outlive the plantation
> Of these long woods of Spanish chestnut and beech.
> For a while over his arable and pasture
> The rooks come idling home. The piled clouds glow
> And fade this late October afternoon.
> Here in his great library, ill and slow,
> He leans between his lamp and the young moon,
> Become the elements of more than nature.

Leslie Hartley was quite different: light-hearted where the other was solemn, alike only in stature and literary skill. He was convivial, enjoying alcohol, and bohemian in the mannerly way of his Edwardian youth. Latterly, he lived in Venice and in Bath, but some of his boyhood had been spent at Hunstanton and it was then, while staying at Bradenham Hall, – when it had been let by the Haggards – that he found himself drawn close to the vortex of his elders' passions. This experience he recounted in his novel, *The Go-Between*, beginning with the memorable words, 'The past is a foreign country: they do things differently there'.

A third contemporary, Arthur Ransome (1884–1967) was an East Anglian but not so deeply embedded in Norfolk as Ketton-Cremer and Hartley, although he was descended from a Quaker miller in Norwich. Ransome was originally a journalist, reporting to the *Manchester Guardian* from Moscow during the First World War, when he played chess with Lenin and married Trotsky's secretary. His journalism was to be overtaken by fiction for children in the *Swallows and Amazons* series of novels, some of which were set on the Broads. Ransome, latterly a Pickwickian figure with white mutton-chop whiskers swagging his rubicund cheeks, caught the dragonfly of childhood imagination on the wing with his stories of voyages and exploration in small boats. Indeed, together with Kenneth Grahame, he fixed the ideal of 'messing about in boats' in the middle-class English ethos. Certainly the Broads themselves, teeming with boat-borne, holidaying families, have never been the same again.

Another contemporary worthy was R. H. Mottram (1883–1971), who chose his native county and Norwich as a background to some of his fiction and Gurney's (later Barclay's) Bank, where he had once worked as a clerk, as a subject. Unlike other Norfolk writers, who relished the privacy offered by its expanse, Ralph Mottram played a vigorous part in the life of Norwich and eventually became its Lord Mayor.

Two other writers, hugely popular in the twentieth century, and with whom the county can claim formative links, could hardly be more different. Anna Sewell (1820–78) is remembered for one novel, *Black Beauty*, the gloriously sentimental story of an ill-used horse. Tradition maintains that the model for 'Black Beauty' was stabled near the author's birthplace in Great Yarmouth, but she left there at the age of two, although thereafter she often stayed on her grandfather's farm at Buxton and the book itself was written at Old Catton in the outskirts of Norwich. Regarded a century after the author's death as a book for children, it was originally written to plead for the better treatment of horses when they were the principal means of transport.

The very different novelist was W. E. Johns (1893–1968), a former sanitary inspector at Swaffham, who became a captain in the Royal Flying Corps and was stationed at the airfield near Narborough during the First World War before being sent to France. His experience of air fighting led to the series of novels – as popular with adolescent boys as *Black Beauty* has been with the girls – about his intrepid hero, Biggles, whose name became a familiar nickname among pilots in the Second World War.

Any survey of twentieth-century writers in Norfolk should

include Sir John Betjeman (1906–84), although he is remembered more easily in Hampstead, Oxford, Cornwall, the City of London and its Metroland suburbs and, indeed, any part of England where the combination of history and architecture inspired him. But he often stayed in the county and particularly cherished two lifelong Norfolk friends, Lady Harrod and Sir Osbert Lancaster. It was near the former's home outside Holt that he visited Letheringsett Hall, a strange house with a portico supported by five giant Doric columns, the former seat of Lord Cozens Hardy. This stirred him to write a haunting poem about the mausoleum on the hill above Letheringsett:

> . . . And even in the summer,
> On a bright East Anglian day
> When round your Doric portico
> Your children's children play
> There's something in the stillness
> And our waiting eyes are drawn
> From the butler and the footman
> Bringing the tea out on the lawn,
> From the little silver spirit lamp
> That burns so blue and still,
> To the half-seen mausoleum
> In the oak trees on the hill . . .

Writers are still drawn to Norfolk but they lack such richness of mood to evoke. The life of the great country houses is not what it was even half a century ago since new occupants may lack roots in the county, or, if they do not, may have withdrawn to an apartment, opening the rest to the public in summer, letting it as flats, or simply shutting it up. Much of the Norfolk that now offers itself to the writer is one of mechanised farming, London's overspill in the suburbs of the towns, holiday cottages empty for most of the year, closes of 'executive homes' on in-fill sites in the villages, caravan parks, drive-in supermarkets and estuaries crowded with white fibreglass yachts. The military historian, Correlli Barnett (b. 1927), whose sharp and controversial study of command in the Second World War, *The Desert Generals*, opened a revisionist offensive, settled in East Carleton and conducted a campaign against the suburbanisation of Norfolk villages with trenchant letters to the *Eastern Daily Press*. But here and there an old house, a wood, or a reach of river touches the imagination as it once touched Rider Haggard's, or John Betjeman's.

At the end of the twentieth century, Norfolk is currently lacking any great, native literary talent. Its most distinguished living historian, Lord Blake (b. 1916), himself a Norfolkman and living at Brundall (and, indeed, a President of the Norfolk Club), seemed to owe more to Oxford, where he was Provost of Queen's College, and to Westminster, which gave him the subjects for books about Disraeli, Salisbury, Bonar Law, Churchill and the Conservative Party.

For him, Borrow's inspiring wind on the heath blew in vain, but he has an historian's understanding of the Norfolk character. This, he first defines as 'non-Celtic' then, more specifically, as

> largely Scandinavian, or Dutch, which is very similar, for there is a lot of Dutch influence in the county. Norfolk people tend to be reserved and suspicious of 'foreigners', by which they mean people from other English counties, especially the 'shires'. Historically, Norfolk, till the railway age, was very remote from London. The journey via Thetford forest was perilous and menaced by highwaymen and the roads were atrocious; it was far easier to go by boat to Holland than by coach to London. It was this remoteness which caused Norwich to be very much an English provincial capital, which in many ways it still is.

Yet the University of East Anglia was proving itself something of a literary seed-bed. The novelist, essayist and playwright, Sir Angus Wilson (1913–91), a Suffolk man himself, was Professor of English Literature there from 1963 to 1978 and founded the university's Master of Arts degree course in 'creative writing'; the novelist and scriptwriter Malcolm Bradbury (b. 1932) was Professor of American Studies from 1970 to 1994 and the poet Anthony Thwaite (b. 1930) was appointed a Writing Fellow in 1972; all this was centred upon the campus around Earlham Hall, once the home of the cultivated Gurneys. Tradition in the Gurney family has it that one of their country neighbours had, some time in the

eighteenth century, been 'the last gentleman who kept a fool'.
A few also kept musicians but the county generated no great
musical tradition and those with that aptitude tended to make
their names elsewhere, much as the organist Charles Burney
moved, as has been seen, to London.

The composer who evokes East Anglia most powerfully is
Benjamin Britten (1913–1976) – who was to become a life
peer, a Companion of Honour and be awarded the Order of
Merit – with his operatic work inspired by the North Sea; yet,
although he lived in Suffolk and founded the Aldeburgh
Festival, Norfolk can claim a little of him for he was educated
by Gresham's School at Holt.

Two Norfolk musicians are, however, remembered. One,
Sarah Glover (1786–1867), the daughter of a Norwich
clergyman and so familiar with church music and choral
singing, made her mark on the teaching of music by inventing
the 'Tonic-Sol-Fa' system that was to inspire the song in *The
Sound of Music*; she herself taught by this method at a school
she and her sister ran in Colegate Street.

A more all-round musician was the Revd Basil Maine
(1894–1972), who, as well as being educated at the City of
Norwich School and dying in retirement at Cromer, made a
national mark as a music critic in Fleet Street and by writing
the biography of his friend Sir Edward Elgar. Maine was not
ordained until he was aged forty-six and thereafter held livings
in Norwich and at Wacton, Warham, Bramerton and
Surlingham, composing a variety of rousing works, including
a waltz for Princess Margaret, an anthem in memory of King
George VI and a birthday march for the Queen Mother.

Basil Maine presided over the Cromer and North Norfolk
Festival of Music and Drama, which, together with those at
King's Lynn and, of course, programmes at Norwich all
through the year, set the pattern for the music festivals which
have since spread throughout the county. These are often of
high quality, such as that started at Burnham Market by Lady
Margaret Douglas-Home, who, as a daughter of Earl Spencer,
spent much of her childhood nearby at North Creake.
Concerts and recitals are now regularly held in great country

houses still in the ownership of the families that built them –
notably at Holkham and Wolterton – and in those now
administered by the National Trust.

As Norfolk has produced its literature, its poetry and its
journalism and some music, so it has produced its visual arts,
both to reflect itself and the world beyond. On the walls of
country houses and weekend cottages, galleries and museums
hang pictures that have as much to convey about the county
and its people as its books.

The literature and art of the county were brought together
by the author of the two-volume work *Portraits in Norfolk
Houses*, yet the author, who studied the art and architecture of
ancient houses and churches and stained glass, was even more
memorable since he seemed to disprove the region's antipathy
to foreigners. In a survey of male society in the Edwardian
period, *Norfolk Leaders: Social and Political*, the antiquary is
placed near the beginning, between the Earl of Leicester and
the Marquess of Lothian, then owner of Blickling. 'A keen
sportsman and a 'Varsity man,' reads the text, he had 'all the
English country gentleman's love of sports of all kinds and
indeed is an adept at all manly exercises, which has added not a
little to his popularity in society. He combines with this a taste
for Art and Archaeology and has made a study of Norfolk
antiquities.' He was also a major in the Norfolk Yeomanry
(with a suitably bristling military moustache), a member of
White's Club in London and was the squire of Blo' Norton
Hall near Thetford. Such was his popularity and erudition that
he was offered a peerage but declined it because he preferred
his inherited title, which was Prince Frederick Duleep Singh
(1868–1926).

The bachelor son of the last Maharajah of the Punjab, who
had been brought to England by Queen Victoria and who had
settled at Elveden Hall – just across the Suffolk border and
transformed by him into an East Anglian vision of a Mogul
palace – 'Prince Freddy' took to English life and the English life
took to him. While his elder brother married a daughter of the
Earl of Coventry, he was content to be a scholarly squire,
writing his monographs and his survey of portraiture. A

fervent monarchist, he hung a portrait of Oliver Cromwell upside down on the wall of his boot-room lavatory. Nearly seventy years after his death, he was recalled by an elderly Norfolk gentleman, who, asked whether his exotic neighbour had been accepted by the county, replied, 'Oh, entirely.'

There, in memory's eye, is a sunburst of paint. It is a painting in oils of a flower – a sunflower, it must be – hanging on the wall of a Norfolk house. It was painted by Sir Matthew Smith and sixty years ago hung in the former pub, where he and his family spent seaside holidays at Burnham Overy Staithe. It was not the sort of painting one came to associate with Norfolk; indeed it was the antithesis of the translucent water-colours of the Norwich School – but it radiated light, and light illuminated the great sweep of countryside from the Wash to the Waveney for artists from that vast bowl of its sky.

It is natural that one thinks of water-colours, so suited to wet and windy landscapes; of 'gifted amateurs' setting up their easels to command some vast arc of vision; or my father with his little black, japanned paint-box glancing up and down as he painted the sea lavender on the salt-marshes into his sketch-book. But water-colours were the invention of the late Georgians and it was other media that reveal the Norfolk and Norfolk people that came before.

The first Norfolk artists are unknown by name. They were craftsmen who twisted the golden torcs for the Iceni and designed the coins and embossed the armour for their Roman conquerors and the invaders who came after. They were followed by the anonymous painters who traced their frescoes on the walls of churches and carved the corbels and gargoyles and the wooden screens and the decorations on the stone fonts and the effigies on the tombs. Sometimes they were foreigners with special skills as painters, sculptors, potters, or goldsmiths.

When the services of portrait-painters were first required they were either summoned to a country house to paint the landowner and his family, or were visited in their London studios; Norfolk was only two days' journey from London, so painters were often available to record the looks of its more prosperous citizens. There were itinerant portrait-painters, too, who stayed at inns and advertised their services by leaflet. These would offer to paint a Yarmouth or Lynn merchant with a trading ship in the background, or a farmer beside his prize bull; some of the most skilful were miniaturists. Occasionally, 'conversation pieces' of a family grouped before their house would be the subject, or even favourite landscapes painted to order. The last of the landscape artists was Edward Pococke (1843–1901), whose innumerable topographical drawings – some of which were published in his *Old and Demolished Norwich* – provide a record of vanished views; they often come up for sale in the county's auction-rooms.

In 1992, a magnificent exhibition of the county's portraiture, called *Norfolk Portraits*, was shown at the Norwich Castle Museum, when its scale and quality became widely apparent. There was Hans Holbein's portrait of Sir John Godsalve of Norwich; Nicholas Hilliard's Sir Thomas Herne of Haveringland; John Hoskins's Le Stranges of Hunstanton; the Townshends of Raynham by Sir Godfrey Kneller; William Hogarth's Cholmondeley family from Houghton; Allan Ramsay's Elizabeth Ann Dering of Hilgay; the Custance family of Weston Longville by Sir William Beechey; Sir Joshua Reynolds's Horace Walpole; Sir Harbord Harbord of Gunton by Thomas Gainsborough; Amelia Opie of Norwich by her husband John Opie; Lord Nelson by Sir William Beechey; Sir Thomas Lawrence's Charles Harvey of Sisted; Henry Cotman by his elder brother John Sell Cotman; Thomas Coke by Richard Reinagle; George Richmond's Elizabeth Fry; Emmeline Le Strange of Hunstanton by George Frederick Watts; Kitty Carr of Ditchingham by William Strang; Augustus John's Admiral Lord Fisher; the Countess of Rocksavage (née Sassoon) by John Singer Sargent; and Edward Seago's Peter Seymour.

These were in addition to Norfolk portraits by less celebrated painters, and portraits by great painters of sitters who were not Norfolk-bred but whose portraits happened to hang in Norfolk houses, while two of the most notable artists, Beechey and Opie, had married Norwich girls and were often in the city.

Of the painters born and bred in Norfolk, or settled there, some produced work of high quality even if not instantly recognisable in the galleries. Fox example, the German-born portrait-painter Theodore Heins (1697–1756) competed for commissions with Thomas Bardwell (1704–67); Joseph Browne (1720–88) began life as a coalman and, on his death, was acclaimed as the 'Norwich Claude', such was his style in painting the imaginary classical landscapes then in fashion. Henry Walton (1746–1813), who lived near the Suffolk border, had studied under Zoffany, from whom he learned the subtleties of painting the 'conversation piece'; his charmingly light, airy and, above all, alive group, *Sir Robert and Lady Buxton with their daughter, Anne*, was the most discussed painting in the 1992 exhibition.

It was not until the end of the eighteenth century that the wide skies, distant landscapes and translucent light of Norfolk brought together a group of like-minded painters who formed a group that achieved world-wide recognition and acclaim. Their medium was often water-colours and they became known as the Norwich School.

The inspiration for the foundation of the first artists' association in provincial England was Joseph Browne and, indeed, their first meetings were held in the house where he himself had worked. In 1803, three years after Browne's death, this informal gathering of local painters, linked by family, friendship, or the study of art, began the convivial, fortnightly meetings of the Norwich Society of Artists. Their first expedition was held in the year of Trafalgar and the Norwich School was to survive, robust yet sensitive and innovative, for three decades.

The pictures they painted were quite different from the romantic canvases of Joseph Browne. Their direct inspiration came from the Norfolk countryside and its reflection of the sky. Their founder was a former errand-boy, who hoped to become an interior decorator, John Crome (1768–1821), who moved away from romantic imaginings to rural realities. His eldest son, John (1794–1842), followed his father's artistic example and, although not his equal as a painter, became even more active in the running of the Society of Artists. His third son, William (1806–67), also became a painter, making up for a lesser talent by adding theatrical or sentimental touches.

But perhaps the archetypical Norwich School painter was John Sell Cotman (1782–1842), who worked in water-colours and captured the play of changing lights on the countryside, pinning it down instantly like butterflies. He spent many years away from Norwich in London and in Great Yarmouth, where he concentrated on etching, but when he returned to the city, in 1806, he was at the peak of his talent as a colourist. His eldest son, Miles (1810–58), who moved to London, followed his father so closely that their work is sometimes confused, while his second son, John, remained in Norwich and took over his father's work as a drawing-master. The Norwich School also included John Thirtle (1777–1839), James Stark (1794–1859), George Vincent (1769–1832) and Joseph Stannard (1797–1830) and they and two dozen others brought to flower the most remarkable manifestation of English landscape-painting.

The Norfolk landscape continued to attract painters in water-colour, amongst them Sir David Murray (1849–1933) and Martin Hardie (1875–1952). A different landscape attracted Howard Carter (1873–1939) away from his native Swaffham. He might, like his father, have become a minor painter and illustrator, inspired particularly by the animals of the Norfolk countryside rather than by the animal-headed gods and goddesses of the Nile Valley. For he, like Rider Haggard before him, had been seduced by the exotic contents of the private museum at Didlington Hall and what began as copying work, recording Lord Amherst's collection of antiquities, led to similar work in archaeology itself. When, in 1923, Carter became the most famous archaeologist of them all with his discovery of the tomb of Tutankhamun, his work as an artist was forgotten. Yet his discovery unleashed an avalanche of artistic activity around the world with the fascination in Egyptian art and architecture.

But it was the same levels, salt-marshes, sands and sea that Carter had left for the heat and glare of the African desert, which inspired some of the next generation of painters and particularly Edward Seago (1910–74) and Peter Scott (1909–89). The former could have made his fortune as a portrait-painter but it was his watery water-colours of the East Anglian shores that sold briskly at annual exhibitions in Bond Street.

The latter, the only son of the Antarctic explorer, Captain Robert Falcon Scott, had been introduced to wildfowling by a contemporary at Cambridge University and, hoping to combine this with his love of painting, looked for a suitable perch on this desolate coast. He found a disused lighthouse – designed by John Rennie, the architect of Waterloo Bridge – on the east bank of the mouth of the river Nene, just over the Lincolnshire border. From here he conducted his shooting and painting expeditions from 1933 until the outbreak of the Second World War, in which he distinguished himself in Light Coastal Forces. He commanded fast gunboats operating mostly in the Channel and North Sea and he painted the flurries of tracer bullets and glare of flares in the night actions on the narrow seas. Before and after the war, his paintings of the birds of the Norfolk saltings were widely reproduced as prints, and even if they did become as hackneyed as china ducks flying across a lounge wall in suburbia, they did capture the energy of their flight and the height and depth of the great spaces in which they flew.

The muted greens, browns, greys, yellows and blues of the Norfolk dunes and salt-marshes did not, however, inspire Sir Matthew Smith (1879–1959), who, like Van Gogh and Cézanne, was drawn to the vivid colours of Provence, and whose blazing sunflower remained in my memory for more than half a century. But, in 1925, he bought a de-licensed pub, The Ship, at Burnham Overy Staithe, as a holiday home for his wife and two young sons. He often visited them there before his wife's death in 1938 and the death of both sons on active service with the RAF during the Second World War. North Norfolk was not, however, for him and the poet Kevin Crossley-Holland wrote of him in his poem, *The Great Painter*,

He has escaped to sweets
At St Colomb, and Paris and Provence,
a plump indulgent wavelength
of pink and crimson, viridian, ultramarine.
The lines here are too Lutheran:
Flat-chested dunes,
the ruled horizontals of marsh and ocean . . .
Not for him
light honed on a northern whetstone,
the burning ice of aurora borealis;
nor was he the first to flinch
at this ruthless incandescence,
too cutting even for Crome and Cotman,
still awaiting a master.

An equally successful painter, albeit in a very different style, Sir Alfred Munnings (1878–1959), remained deeply rooted in East Anglia. A Suffolkman by birth, he was born just south of the Norfolk border at Mendham in the Waveney Valley, the son of a miller. When aged fourteen, he moved to Norwich and there trained to become a poster artist at the Norwich School of Art. He turned to painting in oils and his favourite subjects were horses, whether racing, hunting, hacking or grazing, preferably under wide, bright East Anglian skies. He belonged more to the Newmarket race-course and gallops than anywhere in Norfolk but a major exhibition of his work was held at the Castle Museum. He was a robust character, dressed for the stables like a racing squire with a stock and a hat at a jaunty angle, recalling, perhaps, Surtees; indeed, he wrote three volumes of autobiography and some jocular ballads; his own criticism of modern art was that he would like to kick Picasso in the pants. Nearly 300 of his pictures were exhibited at the Royal Academy of which he became President in 1944, when he was knighted, but he remained a countryman at heart.

One Norfolk artist, a true Norfolkman from the western fenlands, but more at home in London, or the Mediterranean, was Sir Osbert Lancaster (1908–77). His hallmark was wit, whether he was painting townscapes, or scenery for opera or drawing his famous 'Pocket Cartoons' for the *Daily Express*; he was a writer, too, not only of captions for his cartoons but about architecture and his own life and travels. In his memoirs, he drew caricatures of the Edwardian Norfolk of his childhood and his family's home, East Winch Hall.

He always remembered its peace and space and the railway line that was to be his escape to the bustle of the metropolitan world to which he was to belong. 'There is no silence in the world so overwhelming as that which prevails on a small country station when a train has just left,' he wrote in his memoirs, *All Done From Memory*.

> The fact that it is by no means complete, that the fading echoes of the engine are still clearly audible from beyond the signal-box, behind which the guard's van is finally disappearing, that now one hears for the first time the cawing of rooks, a distant dog's bark, the hum of the bees in the station-master's garden, in no way detracts from its quality. The rattling world of points and sleepers, of gossiping fellow-passengers and sepia views of Cromer beach has been whirled away leaving a void which, for some moments yet, the sounds and smells of the countryside will be powerless to fill.

The same village which can claim a share of Sir Matthew Smith was also the holiday choice of another Royal Academician, Robert Austin (1859–1973), a brilliant draughtsman and etcher. He loved water, lived by the Thames at Chiswick and converted a small Primitive Methodist chapel at Burnham Overy Staithe into a residential studio, its main window facing northwards, down the creek to the sea, where he loved to sail. Curiously, Austin was responsible for a striking portrait of Nelson that deserves a place in the iconography of the national hero. In 1943, at the height of the Second World War, the Ministry of Information commissioned morale-building posters of British heroes for railway stations and asked him to portray Nelson. Basing this upon the Lemuel Abbott portrait, which was painted when Nelson was recovering from the loss of his arm and was weak and depressed, Austin, in the interests of wartime morale, added health and vigour to the face, so giving his subject the fire he must have had but which those who painted him from life, when ashore and out of his element, tended to miss.

In the final quarter of the twentieth century, when Norfolk villages filled with redundant businessmen, unemployed actors, middle-class craftsfolk and those seeking escape from cities at weekends, amateur artists of varying abilities produced work to hang in innumerable art exhibitions in village halls. Occasionally, this was of high quality, but usually it was just pleasant, the stuff of charity Christmas cards, reflecting the painter's delight in the surrounding beauty. As the writers discovered, the foreground changes much, the background landscapes and seascapes change little.

Epilogue

If our ancestors could travel into Norfolk at the end of the twentieth century they would, of course, find much altered but also much to recognise. The M11 motorway would whisk them to the border but then, if they strayed off the main roads, they could again wander through lanes between hedgerows and copses, catching distant views of church towers and the pediments, gables and chimney-stacks of country houses above the trees.

They would find it surprisingly difficult to reach any Norfolk port by sea but they could fly to Norwich from Amsterdam. Most of the coast itself would be recognisable: the long sands of the north, the crumbling cliffs around Cromer and the dangerous sandbanks offshore. The core of many villages might have changed little over two centuries but their fringes have often been blighted with the stale formality of suburbia. Norwich, Lynn and Thetford have burst their boundaries over the past half-century as Norfolk's population suddenly expanded: only a little over a quarter of a million at the beginning of the nineteenth century, it had doubled by the outbreak of the First World War and remained almost static until the end of the Second. But between 1951 and 1991 it had increased by about 200, 000 and would be nearly 800, 000 by the end of the century.

Yet here and there remain places where the past seems close. In a country house where an old clock ticks amongst glass cases of stuffed birds; in a neglected church smelling of damp hymn-books; in a wood-framed greenhouse where the vine has broken through the glass; in an unnaturally flat field, where the standing corn gives way to a stretch of cracked concrete that was the hard-standing for a Lancaster bomber half a century ago.

The seasons do not change and, when it snows at Burnham

Thorpe, Nelson's father, the parson, would still find that 'all is Hush at High noon as at Midnight'. There are keen winds in early spring and long, balmy autumns. August, in particular, has been a memorable month in Norfolk. On 4 August 1914, Britain was swept into the First World War; telegraph boys bicycling through the village streets and country lanes bringing the first news of the impending tragedy to a country lazing in summer sunlight. On 1 August 1798, Horatio Nelson of Burnham Thorpe destroyed the French fleet at the Battle of the Nile; he was seen to have changed the course of history overnight and the celebrations began.

On the 196th anniversary of Nelson's victory, it was again tragedy. Early on that warm summer morning, an accidental fire sent Norwich Library up in flames engulfing the great building in minutes. The avenues of shelves where the Colman and Rye collections of Norfolk books were kept and files of county newspapers of the eighteenth and nineteenth centuries, whirled into the sky in columns of ash. Later it became apparent which treasures had been lost, which saved: amongst the former, the memorial library dedicated to the United States Army Air Force of the Second World War; amongst the latter, manuscripts of Sir Rider Haggard's novels and his pencilled journals. News of the disaster was reported by the media as a national catastrophe and even the destruction of the great library of Alexandria was recalled. It was as if Norfolk's memory had suffered a stroke and, if not destroyed, had been gravely impaired.

The tragedy did, however, seem to inspire a stronger determination to remember the past in order to prepare for the future. Local historical societies have become increasingly active, regional histories and monographs were published on an unprecedented scale. An antiquary living near Aylsham took his collection of five hundred books about the county from their shelves and offered them as replacements for those turned to ashes; others were to follow his example. So much had, down the centuries, been forgotten and so much had been wiped from recorded memory in a few minutes' burning, that the act of remembering seemed to become one of the higher virtues.

Bibliography

Armstrong, B. J. *A Norfolk Diary* (2 vols, London, 1949 and 1963).

Astley, H. J. Dukinfield, ed. *Memorials of Old Norfolk* (London, 1908).

Barnes, Pam. *Norfolk Landowners since 1880* (Norwich, 1993).

Bates, Martin. *The Regional Military Histories: East Anglia* (Reading, 1974).

Beatniffe, R. *The Norfolk Tour* (6th ed., Norwich, 1808).

Blomefield, F. *Topographical History of the County of Norfolk* (5 vols, London, 1739–75).

Briers, Frank, ed. *Norwich and its Region* (Norwich, 1961).

Clayton, Joseph. *Robert Kett and the Norfolk Rising* (London, 1912).

Cozens-Hardy, Basil, ed. *The Diary of Silas Neville, 1767–88* (London, 1950).

Crossley-Holland, Kevin. *Waterslain* (London, 1986).

Darroch, Elizabeth and Barry Taylor, eds. *A Bibliography of Norfolk History* (Norwich; Vol. i, 1975; Vol. ii, 1991).

Douglas-Home, Margaret. *A Spencer Childhood* (Saxmundham, 1994).

Dutt, W. A. *Some Literary Associations of East Anglia* (London, 1907).

Dymond, David. *The Norfolk Landscape* (Bury St Edmunds, 1985).

Haggard, Lilias Rider. *I Walked by Night: The Life and History of the King of the Norfolk Poachers* (London, 1935).

——, with Henry Williamson, *Norfolk Life* (London, 1943).

——. *A Norfolk Notebook* (London, 1946).

——. *A Country Scrapbook* (London, 1950).

Haggard, H. Rider. *A Farmer's Year* (London, 1899).

——. *Rural England* (London, 1902).

——. *The Days of My Life* (London, 1926).

Harrod, Wilhelmine. *Norfolk* (London, 1982).

Ketton-Cremer, R. W. *Norfolk Portraits* (London, 1944).

——. *A Norfolk Gallery* (London, 1948).

——. *Norfolk Assembly* (London, 1957).

——. *Forty Norfolk Essays* (Norwich, 1961).

——. *Felbrigg* (London, 1962).

——. *Norfolk in the Civil War* (London, 1969).

Land, Paul K. *Kett's Rebellion* (Ipswich, 1977).

Linnell, Charles. *Some East Anglian Clergy* (London, 1961).

Margeson, Sue (with Fabienne Seillier and Andrew Rogerson). *The Normans in Norfolk* (Norwich, 1994).

Matcham, M. Eyre. *The Nelsons of Burnham Thorpe* (London, 1911).

McCrery, Nigel. *The Vanished Battalion* (London, 1992).

Moore, Andrew (with Charlotte Crawley). *Family and Friends: a Regional Survey of British Portraiture* (London, 1992).

Paul, Leslie. *Heron Lake* (London, 1948).

Pocock, Guy. *Period Programme* (London, 1936).

Pocock, Tom. *Remember Nelson: The Life of Captain Sir William Hoste* (London, 1977).

——. *Horatio Nelson* (London, 1987).

——. *Rider Haggard and the Lost Empire* (London, 1993).

Roberts, C. V. and D. P. Mortlock. *Popular Guide to Norfolk Churches* (3 vols, Cambridge, 1981–5).

Rye, Walter, *A History of Norfolk* (London, 1885).

Sager, Peter. *East Anglia* (London, 1990).

Scott, Clement. *Poppy-Land* (Norwich, 1886).

Seymour, John. *The Companion Guide to East Anglia* (London, 1970).

Skipper, Keith. *The Norfolk Connection* (Norwich, 1991).

Smith, Graham. *Norfolk Airfields in the Second World War* (Newbury, 1994).

Stirling, A. M. W. *Coke of Norfolk and His Friends* (London, 1908).

Turner, E. L. *Bird Watching on Scolt Head* (London, 1928).

Wade Martins, Peter. *An Historical Atlas of Norfolk* (Norwich, 1993).

Wade Martins, Susanna. *A History of Norfolk* (Chichester, 1984).

Wallace, Doreen and R. P. Bagnall-Oakley. *Norfolk* (London, 1951).

William, N. J. *The Maritime Trade of East Anglian Ports* (Oxford, 1988).

Williamson, Henry. *The Story of a Norfolk Farm* (London, 1941).

Williamson, Tom. *The Origins of Norfolk* (Manchester, 1993).

Woodforde, J. *The Diary of a Country Parson, 1758–81* (5 vols, London, 1924–31).

Yaxley, David. *Portrait of Norfolk* (London, 1977).

Index